Gardens for the Soul

Gardens for the Soul

Designing outdoor spaces
using ancient symbols,
healing plants, and feng shui

Pamela Woods

Photography by
John Glover

Foreword by
Gina Lazenby

RIZZOLI
NEW YORK

First published in the United States of America in 2002 by
RIZZOLI INTERNATIONAL PUBLICATIONS, INC.
300 Park Avenue South
New York, NY 10010

ISBN 0-8478-2478-0

First published in the United Kingdom in 2002 by
Conran Octopus Limited
Text copyright © Pamela Woods 2002
Book design and layout copyright
© Conran Octopus 2002

Publishing Director: Lorraine Dickey
Senior Editor: Muna Reyal
Project Editor: Kate Haxell

Creative Manager: Lucy Gowans
Designer: Lucy Holmes
Picture Manager: Liz Boyd

Production Manager: Adam Smith
Senior Production Controller: Manjit Sihra

Printed in China

Contents

Foreword

This beautiful book could be a very exciting experience for you. The photographs are certainly breathtaking, but what I feel will inspire you is the awareness of how important a role your garden plays in your life. Perhaps you had not realized before just how much that green plot outside your back door could make a huge contribution to your health at all levels, physical, emotional, mental – and your spiritual well-being.

Over the last decade I have really made a study of what it takes to be healthy. My interest in this came about because I wanted to get well and recover from an illness triggered by overwork, loss of focus and stress. I had a resistance to taking prescribed medication, so I set off on a journey to find out how I could help myself get back into balance. I learned so much about myself – who I was, what drove me, what was important to me. It became a search for the sacred within my life. I discovered I had a spiritual hunger.

Eventually I realized that I needed a stronger connection with the natural world. I started to yearn for a closer connection with nature – something beyond the window boxes outside my mews house in central London. I needed to see big horizons, endless skies and I knew I wanted to be in a garden. I started to recognise how much healing I could get from being with plants, trees and grass.

I know I am not the only one who has experienced a moment of questioning what their life is about. More and more people are beginning to do that, asking themselves questions about what is really important to them. Ultimately the answers about meaning all lie within us, but to make that connection most of us need some kind of support or trigger. The natural world holds the key to guiding us back to a more natural way of being and feeling. What better way than to experience nature and the wonders of the natural world than in your own garden.

In this exquisite book, Pamela reminds us that answers come from nature and the doorway to spiritual nourishment is in our garden. It is so simple! I know I have travelled thousands of miles visiting other countries, cultures, communities and people, asking questions, searching for clues about what direction to steer my life. And I found that all I had to do was to come home and walk outside my own front door to commune with my own little corner of this huge planet.

I feel passionate about making a difference in the world, that's why I loved writing my books on feng shui and healthy homes. I wanted to help people with information that I strongly believe will have a positive impact on their lives. What I have learned about changing the world is that we can't change anything except ourselves.

I remember a quote about Mother Teresa. When asked how to bring peace to the world she answered that we should go home and love our family. The simple, and yet profound idea that we can influence others only by what we do. All we can do is put our own house in order. It means that we have to examine our attitudes, judgements, prejudices, motivations and our capacity for love. And to do so requires a quiet, peaceful and loving heart. Where better to find this than in nature and our own sacred garden.

In showing us how to connect more deeply with ourselves and with our gardens, Pamela has created a powerful tool to support our personal transformation. The real gift of this book is what Pamela is able to share of herself and her work. Her passion and love of gardens come shining through.

This is no ordinary gardening tome. I love this book and, speaking as one who doesn't know the first thing about weeding, digging or planting, I was truly inspired to get out there and have a go. I shall let Pamela's book guide me in shaping our garden into the sanctuary that we would love to have.

GINA LAZENBY

Introduction

This book is written for both the gardener and for the seeker of the sacred in nature. Its purpose is to reveal the hidden reasons behind the creation of gardens of great beauty, to cast light on the sources of their design and to discover why they have come to be sacred gardens.

I am often asked, 'What is a spirit or sacred garden?' The word 'sacred' means different things to different people, but for me the meaning comes from a strong sense that communing with Nature is akin to contact with the Divine. To some, the Divine may be called God, to others it may simply be referred to as the Life Force. For those in a love affair with nature, gardening can be no less than a taste of heaven itself.

Through the pages of this book I want to encourage you to take a journey through your personal inner world, so that your own spiritual landscape emerges clearly in readiness for its physical realization in your garden. I will explain the many ways in which you can include sacred symbols – even in the smallest garden schemes, anywhere in the world – and inspire you with the magic of the wild landscape.

We live in an age when a growing number of people are just beginning to explore the realms of the sacred in their lives. This 'awakening' is coinciding with a great surge of anxiety about the state of the Earth – our home. At the same time, there has been a renewed fascination with the making of gardens and, indeed, another great gardening renaissance is upon us. The spirit garden is emerging as part of this movement.

The beautiful forms and patterns of sacred symbols are universal metaphors for spiritual harmony and, if you allow them to, they can exert a powerful force on your own sacred space and even on your everyday life. I want to help the first-time gardener to experiment with weaving sacred aspects into their schemes, while more experienced gardeners may find a way to deepen the expression and meaning of their gardens.

Journey of discovery

I have been an artist and gardener for many years, so becoming a garden designer was a natural progression. What I didn't expect was to feel a restlessness and dissatisfaction with my work as a designer in the traditional school of garden design. Creating purely aesthetically pleasing gardens became no longer enough for me.

I began to travel more and more, and it was from the truly wild places that I started to draw renewed inspiration for my work. As a child, I was always happiest when left to wander among nature, and as an adult, travelling further and further afield, including China, India and Australia, my mind began to open up to the meaning and significance of the marks and patterns made by people on the landscape.

I was struck by the gracious beauty of the Taj Mahal gardens at Agra, in India, but was more intrigued – as I wandered along the dusty tracks of the Indonesian island of Bali – to discover the sacred courtyard shrines built within the gardens of almost every home that I passed. Honouring the Spirits is an everyday activity for the ordinary Balinese people.

During one particular journey to Australia I found myself profoundly moved by the sacred power and beauty of Uluru (Ayers Rock). This huge outcrop of red sandstone, found in the centre of vast deserts, is reached after travelling across hundreds of miles of flat plain, and nothing could have prepared me for the impact its awesome presence made on me.

The Aborigines hold that their land is peppered with sacred places connected by 'Songlines'. The tribal initiates learn these 'songs' from their elders and ancestor-spirits and can then travel the continent via these invisible, sacred maps. Only the land can reveal the songs, and the act of walking upon it is considered sacred. Clearly, this information has very practical benefits when travelling the endless deserts of the Outback, but

Left Silvery light,
pouring through
an arched gateway
onto late summer
herbaceous borders
in Gertrude Jekyll's
summer garden at
Munstead Wood,
Surrey, England.
Here, surrounded by
the beautiful planting
of a great garden artist,
the lover of plants and
gardens can sense the
sacredness in her work.

Top The Aborigines believe Uluru to be the 'Belly of the Mother'. Being there gave me a new awareness of the Earth as the container of wisdom and mysterious spiritual teachings.
Above Glastonbury is one of the ancient, sacred sites of Britain and, along with the stone temple of Avebury, is one of the points through which the Michael and Mary ley lines travel.

to the deeply spiritual Aborigines, the Songlines also have a much greater significance that permeates through their whole culture.

On returning to Britain, I discovered that the Songlines of the Aborigines could be compared to the ancient ley lines of my own country. Such lines were first described in the 1920s by the photographer and businessman, Alfred Watkins. He felt he had traced remnants of a prehistoric land-tracking system, marked in later times by the positions of sacred sites and ancient churches.

These lines have also been extensively described in a fascinating book called *The Sun and the Serpent*. It traces in detail two main 'routes', the Michael and the Mary lines, that travel in parallel from the tip of Cornwall to East Anglia, through many ancient sites in Britain.

As I travelled some of the ancient pathways of the world and contemplated a time when people were more in tune with the spiritual reality of the landscape, I saw a new style of design work emerge in me. I felt a closer interaction with the subtleties of the landscape and the garden owners themselves. I began to propose the building of more meaningful gardens, where the sacred act of placing one's feet and hands on the land could once more come alive.

Inspiration from the past

Your own spirit garden can be created using the inspiration provided by any number of personal spiritual experiences. Sometimes, however, it is helpful to travel back through time to seek inspiration from the work of our ancestors.

The Moorish 'Paradise' gardens were inspired by the teachings of the Koran. The gardens were often divided into four sections, symbolizing the way Paradise was divided by four rivers. The central point of the garden was said to be where God and man could meet. Water, in the form of rills, pools and fountains, played a special part in the making of a Moorish Paradise.

intersecting pathway that made the sign of the cross, with a well or fountain marking the centre.

Another typical feature was the 'flowery mead', not unlike today's wildflower garden. This area was full of flowers and grasses that could be used to decorate the church or make medicines.

The Japanese gardens that we see today are the latest in the country's long line of spiritual gardening traditions. In Japan, centuries before Zen Buddhism became established, the ancient Shinto religion of Nature-worship mingled with Chinese Taoist teachings and told how Spirits could be encouraged to come down to the human realm through the creation of beautiful gardens. With lakes, islands and lush plantings, these gardens were heaven on earth.

The designs of the Christian monastic gardens of medieval Europe, the Zen Buddhist gardens within the walled monastery courtyards of Kyoto in Japan and the Islamic Paradise gardens were expressions of a particular view of the Universe. Their beauty and purpose were ways of affirming the philosophies that they sprang from. However, I feel sure that the spiritual devotees tending these sacred spaces also benefited in other ways from the very earthy occupation of working in their gardens.

Contemporary designers

Some of today's garden artists and designers, particularly those who are working in the international arena, are increasingly often requested to incorporate various different ancient belief systems into their designs and to create places that celebrate both a country's history and a feeling of spiritual universality. One such artist and designer is an American, Kathryn Gustafson. She has created some of the most exciting new public spaces in the world, and, in the troubled land of Lebanon, has designed a Garden of Forgiveness, or *Hadiquat-as-Samah*, at an ancient site within Beirut city.

Above The Zen garden style known as the *karesansui*, or dry landscape, is highly minimalist. It aims to capture the essence of the natural landscape – its mountains, rivers, forests, plains and oceans – through careful placing of specially chosen rocks, raked gravel and a simple scattering of plants. The simplicity and the clear, open spaces are symbolic of the stripping away of the mind's delusions to reveal the sublime nature of reality.

Today, marvellous examples of these gardens can still be found in Spain, across Asia and in Northern India, the most famous sites being the Alhambra Palace Gardens in Granada and the Taj Mahal. These strikingly designed and finely executed gardens are still places of great beauty and pleasure, where symmetry, mathematical perfection and sacred plants are artistically woven into extravagant oases.

The medieval monks of the Christian orders across Europe created monastery gardens of a very different style, but as in the Moorish gardens, the overall layout was loaded with spiritual meaning. Monastery gardens were also commonly divided into four parts, this time by an

This sunken garden holds layers of Byzantine, Greek, Roman, Islamic and Ottoman ruins and bears the marks of the recent civil wars. The new design aims to integrate all these remains by using what Kathryn calls a visual language of metaphors for unity. She is known for her capacity to work responsively and intuitively with the landscape.

While Kathryn Gustafson creates an intimate experience through her apparently easy but vast 'land sculpting', Dan Pearson's genius is expressed in his relationship with plants. For him, the movement of time and the seasons help to put him in touch with his own spirituality.

Dan's commission to redesign the island at Althorp, Princess Diana's final resting place, and the memorial garden that leads to it, was carried out with a characteristically light touch. He says that it was impossible to ignore the symbolism of his work there.

He simplified and revitalized the landscape approaching the Round Oval with a green meadow full of long grasses and English wild flowers. One hundred white rambling roses were planted on the island and allowed to scramble over its trees and shrubs. A striking 'ribbon' of grass flanks the island's banks and he also fringed the lake with wild rushes and imported dozens of white water lilies to grow there.

Many other artists have created landscapes with a strong sense of individual magic and personal sacredness. In making his shingle garden on the bleak coastline of Dungeness, in Kent, England, the film director and artist, Derek Jarman, very privately created a unique garden. He positioned wind- and salt-tolerant plants among the artistry of carefully placed flotsam and jetsam, and the whole garden became the backdrop of the poetry that he wrote in his last years.

The unfolding of time, as seen in the natural cycle of the seasons, is central to the works and writings of many artists creating designs for the garden and the wider landscape.

In his book *Time*, natural artist and photographer, Andy Goldsworthy, speaks of the value he places on the slow movement of the seasons at home in Scotland, and how much he resents 'jumping' into another landscape further south where he hasn't been privy to the unfolding of the leaves he can see on the trees. It is not surprising, then, that much of his recent work has centred on observing the subtle effects of time and the tides.

Dream source

Passionate gardeners often have a special garden that fills them with inspiration every time they visit or conjure it in their imagination. It may be a garden they knew as a child, a landscape from their travels, a perfect feeling or even a dream. In my design work, the biggest challenge is to help my clients discover something of their 'dream garden'.

Designing a spirit garden involves my drawing directly from their personal dream source. Each of us has an inner landscape we can tap into when creating a sacred space and this is also capable of feeding and nourishing our inner world.

In writing this book I became aware of the challenge of balancing the two sides of my work – the rational and practical with the inspired and creative. The task has often felt akin to that of the medieval alchemists, who in balancing and uniting opposing forces were attempting to create something ultimately more precious than gold.

Carl Jung studied the human psyche and called the garden a metaphor for the soul and a place of multi-foliate imagery. He believed that symbols of the garden could appear to us in our dreams.

The garden in mythology has always been viewed as a sacred, magical and potent place where spiritual adventures can take place and I see the creation of a spirit garden as a significant and magical act! Whether you view yourself as an artist or as a gardener, you may, through the pages of this book, become inspired to include an expression of sacredness in your own garden.

Above Derek Jarman's unique mandala-like garden and his love of plants express to me his longing for a return to England's lost past. Taken in mid-summer, while he was still alive, this photograph shows the driftwood sculpture garden that Derek was always adding to with found objects from the sea. This most soulful and individual expression within a garden has created what is for me one of our most significant contemporary spirit gardens.

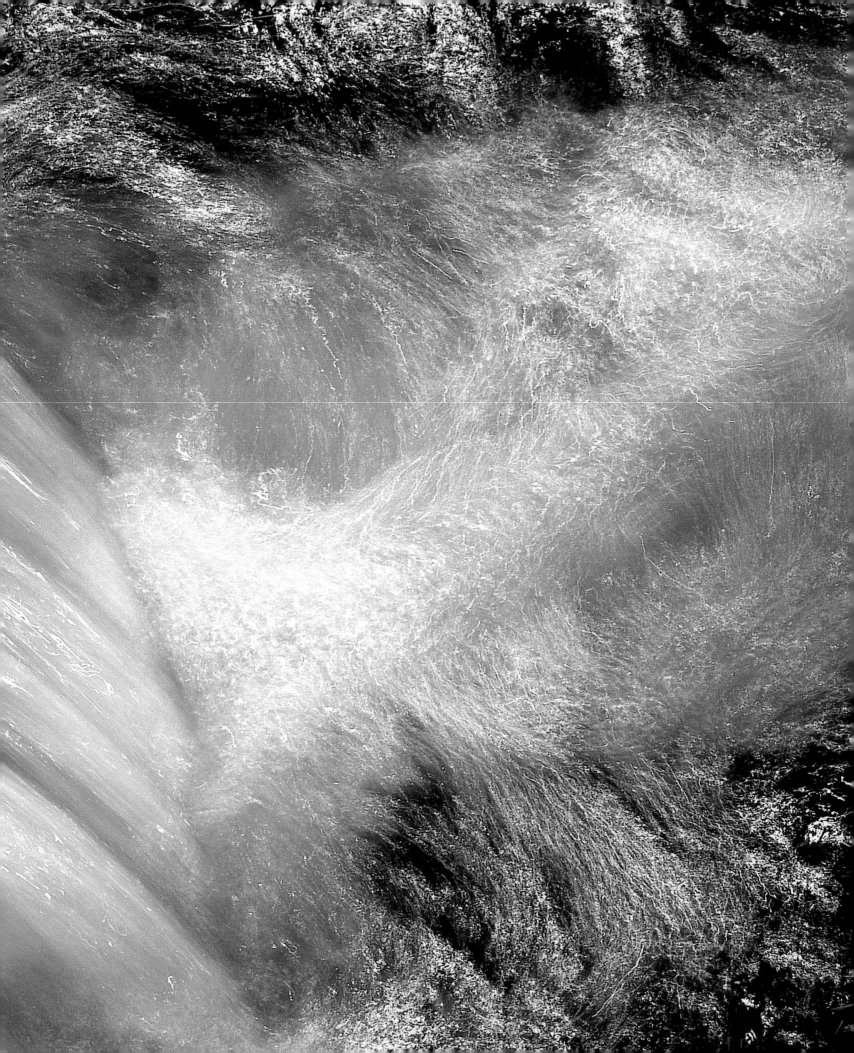

The energy within a garden is created by highly visible elements, such as fast-moving water, together with softer, more subtle factors, such as light and colour and even the unseen forces of the earth beneath our feet.

Garden energy

Energy in the garden

Above The invisible energy of air becomes visible in the form of the moving leaves of plants in the garden. Here, in a garden designed by Land Art at the Hampton Court Palace Flower Show, verbascums, grasses, achilleas and foxtail lilies, dance in the gentle breeze.

Right A misty morning experience of the herbaceous borders at Parham Park, West Sussex, England. At this time of day, the colour and architectural quality of these plants, evoke an especially mysterious and gentle energy.

The word 'energy' means many different things to different people, but it is usually understood to be some kind of unseen force. Scientists routinely discuss such things as electricity and sound waves, which are forms of energy that are measurable and are able to be manipulated, even though they are invisible. Likewise, there seem to be many more waves and vibrations that emanate from living and so-called inert matter that can be felt or in some way measured, although you can not see them.

In the garden, it is important to try to become attuned to the kinds of energy that are present, because different kinds can create different atmospheres. Some of these atmospheres appear to assist the contemplation of spirit, whilst others do not. For instance, a garden that is set beside a busy road will be affected by a certain sort of ambient energy that may well be highly distracting in the contemplation of the natural world.

It is helpful to learn how to distinguish between the different forms of energy so that you can create a garden containing the fine and subtle qualities you desire.

Energy in the sacred garden is everything, and the energy within the garden is created by everything contained in it. This is another way of saying that to create a sacred garden space, everything intended for it needs to be selected and sited with care and with reference to the existing energy flow.

Each of us has an instinctive understanding and awareness of energy flow, but as human beings in this modern age, we have largely forgotten how to use such knowledge. To compound this, most of us find the words available to describe these kinds of energies obscure or even off-putting. However, I feel that their rediscovery is fundamentally important in the appreciation and creation of beautiful gardens. I want to explore this in some depth in this chapter.

Energy trackways and sacred sites

Right and below The shadow path cast by the Mother Stone, the biggest and most sculptural stone in the circle at Castlerigg. This stone was used to mark the midsummer setting sun and was erected at the edge of a long straight slope in the hillside in order to project its dead straight shadow for over a mile down the valley. The line of this alignment/ shadow path was plotted across the landscape and was found to be a significant ley line.

Far right Castlerigg is one of the most beautiful examples of an ancient megalithic site. It stands on raised ground with a magnificent view of the high fells which completely encircle it, forming a vast amphitheatre. Thus the stone circle is the sacred centre of this natural landscape mandala.

We know from both traditional and modern medicine that our bodies contain complex micro trackways – the meridians – that have energy flowing through them. Landscape 'energy' describes what is otherwise an invisible charge, not unlike that travelling through the body, and which we can sometimes sense in wild or ancient landscapes that have a powerful energy signature.

Many of the ancient churches and places of Christian worship are built on what were sacred pagan sites, which stood where land energy was strong. It seems that the ancestral peoples were far more in tune with the Earth's subtle energies than we are today, and they passed on their knowledge to each succeeding generation. In doing so, they maintained the sacred rituals that affirmed and celebrated the energy of the land.

Today's sacred sites that mark ancient points of particularly strong 'energy' are usually places with a special spiritual history. As gardeners, there is much we can learn about energy by visiting them. Tracks of energy, known in Britain as ley lines, which were noted by the peoples of prehistory, link these sacred sites together as they travel for many miles across the landscape.

In the 1930s, The Old Straight Track Club, inspired by the writings of Alfred Watkins in his *Ley Hunters Manual*, took outings to these sites and followed the tracks to places of special significance. These included wells, standing stones, ancient churches and stone circles, such as the one at Castlerigg, near Keswick in Cumbria, England, which is shown on these pages. The club's members were seeking to learn how the energies of these places were subtly different.

The most recent thinking about these lines is that they are, in fact, spirit lines that allow the spirit of the shaman to travel across the sacred landscape. Although the landscape is marked by standing stones or circles, the energy at these sites can only be truly experienced by the released spirit of the shaman or devotee.

Spirit of place

In England, the awesome energy of Stonehenge, in Wiltshire, at the winter solstice contrasts strikingly with the intimate and feminine atmosphere of the Chalice Well Gardens near Glastonbury, in Gloucestershire, at midsummer. Both these places are an expression of the ancient spiritual tradition of the British Isles, and yet they are very different.

Stonehenge stands upright and bleak in the surrounding landscape, visible for miles around and seeming to speak of an awesome cosmic force. In contrast, the Chalice Well Gardens are a cluster of tiny intimate places, secret little bowers with delicate flowers and ferns gathered around the gently flowing spring water. Clearly, the builders of these places were sensitive to the energy that existed at each site and also had strong ideas about what they wanted to celebrate or evoke.

The Chalice Well Gardens are visited by people wishing to take the waters for healing, but they also provide a special place for meditation on the divine feminine force, otherwise known as the Goddess. The element of water is said to be akin to the feminine spirit, and here water abounds in the form of a flow of iron-rich water from the sacred Red Spring that moves from one end of the garden to the other, coating all it touches with a film of beautiful red iron oxide.

Gardens have served as sanctuaries for millennia, as places of peace, tranquillity and contemplation. They call forth a deep stillness and can lead to a feeling of wholeness. Today, they serve as an escape from hectic, modern-day living and as a place to return to the magic of nature. A visit to Chalice Well Gardens always refreshes my spirit and renews my belief that creating a sacred garden is the perfect way of honouring the spirit of the Earth.

When I was travelling in Victoria, Australia, I came across a unique garden known as the William Rickets Sanctuary. This most sacred place holds the extraordinary work of a sculptor – the eponymous William Rickets – who lived to his late nineties, and for a period of his life lived with the Central Australian Aborigines. He was privileged to be initiated into their spiritual ways, and he learned that the Aborigines see themselves and their land as inseparably joined, with the land holding all their ancestor-beings.

Within the Sanctuary is an evocative collection of sculptures, some set on massive rocks and many with water bubbling over their mossy surfaces, bringing them to life. As I stepped through the wooded garden, time seemed to stand still as each exquisite and tenderly made piece was slowly revealed. The feelings I experienced within this garden assured me of the artist's intention to touch the visitor with the spiritual wealth of the Aborigines.

Modern man is only just beginning to recognize the prodigious knowledge held by indigenous peoples about their native landscapes and to tap into their ancient wisdom. As a designer of gardens with a quest for beauty, I value the wild places to put me in touch with what I feel to be my own wild or indigenous soul.

Right People come to Chalice Well to see the gardens and take the waters. Here in the area known as Arthur's Court, a little waterfall pours gently over the rocks, past ferns and ivy and further on into an ancient bathing pool. This particular part of the garden is especially feminine in nature and offers the visitor the chance to stay a while and contemplate the qualities of the Goddess contained within it.

'Dreaming in' the energy of the garden

Below Iris sibirica and *Stipa tenuissima* surround this intriguing 'dreaming pool', placed in the *Gardens Illustrated* garden for The Chelsea Flower Show 2000, designed by Piet Oudolf and Arne Maynard. The pool bowl has a reflective metal surface, the base of which is intermittently struck with a hammer to make concentric circular ripples and give a dreamlike, bubbling look to the water.

Right Fall in Maine, USA; a band of mist hangs between the trees and the mountains. This is a vast wilderness landscape and at this time of year the autumn colour stretches as far as the eye can see across the valleys and mountains – an unforgettable sight that exemplifies the extraordinary, overwhelming beauty of Nature.

When you set out to create a garden of the spirit, you need to ask yourself what qualities already exist within the garden and what qualities you wish to evoke. You don't need to know why you want them: it is often best to follow your heart's desire and try to make sense of it all later.

In developing a spirit garden at Broxmore in Hampshire, England, Robert Seaton was keen to follow his heart and incorporate energy techniques he'd read about in Michaela Small Wright's book *Co-Creative Science*. In this, the author, a scientist who writes about her hands-on experience of working with nature intelligences, describes in a very down-to-earth manner how humans can co-operate with the energies of nature and plants.

Robert followed her suggested first step and wrote down a detailed and heart-felt 'intent', in which he described his wishes for the garden. He gave me this to work with before I started on the design. Michaela asserts that the writing of this intent is a magical or energetic act, and I felt that this was the beginning of the creation of a very unusual garden, one with a will of its own.

Broxmore is a walled, one-acre garden and the high walls not only create a sheltered microclimate, but also assist in containing the atmosphere of this spirit garden.

If a well is found, I feel it should be preserved, to keep the energy of the underground water mixing with the air. Broxmore has a well at its very centre, and this has become the main focus of the design. To emphasize its tremendous significance, we placed around it a beautiful rose-covered meditation arbour.

I have found that dreams and daydreams, if listened to, can contain valuable, if subtle, information about the energy that is either present or needed in a garden. While I was designing Robert's garden, I experienced vivid dreams of particular plants – most memorably irises – which have now become an important element in the garden.

Feeling wilderness energy

Many gardeners find inspiration in an untamed landscape. Places as diverse as the Amazon rainforest and the Scottish Highlands draw us to explore, but we might be equally captivated and enriched by a local hillside or a hedgerow in a country lane. Landscapes hold different spiritual characteristics that can touch our emotions.

I encourage my clients, when seeking to create their own sacred garden, to take special note of these feelings and observe where they are when they arise. A closer relationship with your responses in these wild places may reveal a deep 'soul connection' and a potential source of a very personal inspiration for the design of your garden and maybe, indeed, for your life itself.

In the creation of a sacred garden, we seek to understand the existing energy of the site and also to create a particular energy or atmosphere of our own choosing – perhaps one where we will be able to sense the presence of the Divine. Many clues we need for this process may well be found in the observation of the energy in wild places.

Shifting a city garden's energy

Left Broxmore garden already had high, mellowed and aged brick walls that enclosed the garden, 'holding' the energy in place. While this type of physical enclosure is not always needed, it can be essential if the garden space is imposed upon by disruptive outside energy sources.

Right Mary Rose Moss's city garden is surrounded by tall buildings, but by enclosing it with traditional trelliswork, we created privacy and relocated the energy closer to the ground. The lovely arbour and seat give Mary Rose somewhere to sit and dream among the scent of the climbing roses and the many bees collecting pollen from the flowers of monarda, thymes and lavenders.

As a garden designer, I am always challenged to respond to different energy problems. On first visiting a site, I search intently for the key energy factor, which if adjusted, could make the transformation into a garden sanctuary possible.

When I visited Mary Rose Moss's courtyard garden on the edge of Primrose Hill, in London, England, I was struck by the height of the buildings around it. Here was a garden without any privacy, dwarfed by the surrounding man-made structures. The garden is reached by climbing a set of steep steps from the ground floor and from here both the eye and the energy are directed skywards.

I felt that the focus of attention needed to be drawn downwards to the ground instead, and that an enclosure was vital to contain the space and the garden's energy. Mary Rose wanted to keep the existing central water feature and to have places where she could lay out part of her collection of exquisite crystals. This was her first garden and she was keen to learn about plants and how to care for them. She also wanted a garden of peace and beauty as a sanctuary from

her busy working life in the City. She had very clear ideas about the colour scheme she wanted – soft pastels, including pinks, blues and mauves, lemons, creams and white.

I designed a traditional trelliswork screen, to be positioned within, and above, the existing lower brick-wall enclosure. A trelliswork arbour was also made, containing a timber seat. Mary Rose had told me that she didn't expect to sit in her garden very often, but I felt that the private space that an arbour creates might encourage her to do so. These structures, stained a gentle blue-green, covered the dark brickwork and worked beautifully with the soft-coloured plantings.

The selection and placing of plants and the creation of an enclosure brought about the necessary shift of energy, so that it is now 'held' comfortably within the garden space. Even in the first year, and with all the disruption of the building work, the garden was full of summer flowers and alive with the energy of bees. Its positive effect has been such that Mary Rose has now truly acquired that familiar gardening obsession.

The energy of a garden paradise

In complete contrast to the little London courtyard on the previous pages, in both scale and style, are the Gardens of Montserrat near Sintra, in Portugal. William Beckford (1760–1844), an eccentric English writer and collector, with a liking for the Gothic in his literature, art and architecture, bought the gardens in the eighteenth century.

He commissioned a leading horticultural specialist of the day to recreate an English paradise, an enclosure with an other-worldly atmosphere. Together with his friend, the poet Byron, he left the social constraints of life in eighteenth-century England and created a garden that is both magical and inspiring. Even today, the garden generates an incredibly powerful atmosphere.

An English meadow was recreated – originally even sheep were shipped in from England to complete the picture – and beautifully positioned trees 'hung' on the hillside. I discovered the most magical areas in the woods and near the streams and pools. Water travels continuously through the garden, giving a wonderful sense of the flowing energy of life. A mock-Gothic ruin, hidden in the trees, felt to me to be alive with wood spirits. Stone-carved, wand-like sculptures with ancient

patternings look as though they are 'growing' among the ferns, and a surreal and ornately decorated garden house, set on the hillside, can be seen through breaks in the trees.

The creation of Arcadian gardens, or the Paradise Landscape, eclipsed even the Gardens of Montserrat. They saw the naturalizing of the landscape and the movement away from the formal, geometric and mathematically calculated design of gardens.

William Kent (1686–1748), an architect, interior designer and landscape designer, travelled to Europe in 1716 and observed the landscape paintings of Salvator Rosa, Nicolas Pousin and Claude Lorraine. He returned to England holding the dream of Elysian Fields, distant temples, grottoes and splendid trees, which he translated into elegant Palladian gardens such as Rousham in Oxfordshire, England.

Painshill Park, near Cobham, Surrey, England, was the vision of Charles Hamilton (1704–1786), a painter, plantsman and a highly talented land-scape designer. It still holds the essence of the English paradise garden era, and here the true dream of that time can still be experienced.

Far left Painshill Park is one of Europe's finest 18th-century landscape gardens. Charles Hamilton transformed what was considered at the time to be a barren heathland, into ornamental pleasure gardens, which also contain a vinery and a unique crystal grotto. After falling into disrepair from 1948, the park is now undergoing a faithful restoration and is a magical place in which to wander and experience the 18th-century idea of paradise.

Left The view through the three church-like windows of the Gothic Temple, looking towards the lake.

Feng shui

Above This hand-crafted green oak and bamboo 'Moon Gate', created by James Showers following my own design, formed the entrance to The Feng Shui Garden at Hampton Court Palace Flower Show. As in traditional Chinese gardens, the Moon Gate, which is slightly low, is intended to make visitors bow as they enter the garden. It marks the entry point, where one can decide to slip out of everyday awareness and become conscious of stepping into a finer and sacred space where the spirits have also been invited to visit.

Feng shui, which literally means 'wind and water', is the ancient Chinese science of understanding our relationship with the forces of life and the way we interact with them to proceed in our destiny. There are several schools of feng shui and many different approaches to understanding energy through them, but their central purpose is to bring about balance and harmony, which in turn will encourage our well-being and prosperity.

In 1999, while building a feng shui garden at Hampton Court Palace Flower Show, I was approached by a Chinese man, who told me the origins of feng shui. According to this, in ancient times, the Chinese believed there was a beautiful garden in the heavens where immortals dwelled.

A certain Emperor decided to make a garden just as exquisite for himself, on Earth. It would contain all the qualities of beauty, balance and harmony needed to attract the spirits. This would enable the Emperor to rub shoulders with the immortals whenever he wished. The call was sent out all over the land for the best gardeners to come forward, but before their task could begin, a guide was needed so that they would be able to work with the energy and spirit of the land – this guide is the ancient art of feng shui.

This tale can help us to step away from all of the confusion surrounding feng shui. It encourages us to understand that, by creating beauty, we are attracting the spirits needed to enrich our lives.

The Chinese have a very long tradition of describing the subtleties of the Earth's energy and are, indeed, masters of this field of study, in medicine, landscaping and the esoteric arts.

Energy, or *chi*, otherwise known as the Life Force or 'Dragon's Breath', is said to be manifest within the Five Elements of earth, fire, water, wood and metal, which make up the very material of earthly existence. Each element is held to pertain to a particular colour, season and aspect of life.

Feng shui can be a useful design tool in the creation of balance and beauty in a garden. As Sheila Lister, a feng shui consultant, says, 'A sacred garden is one which naturally uses the principles of feng shui, and feng shui is naturally used in the creation of a sacred garden'. By this, she means that whether you consciously or unconsciously use feng shui, a beautifully balanced and well-designed garden would naturally demonstrate these principles.

The flow of *chi*

The presence and flow of water is a factor of great significance in feng shui. The free flow of *chi* is said to encourage our well-being, so a stagnant pond in the garden could be seen as an example of something which needs to be balanced and rejuvenated by being cleaned out and, perhaps, by adding a fountain.

Air flow is also very significant and any gardener knows the benefits of healthy air movement around plants. If, however, the movement is too strong or turbulent, beneficial energy can be disrupted and depleted – think of how you feel sitting in a persistent, cold draught – an example of what is known as *sha chi*. Again, in feng shui, enclosure is an important energy factor in the design of a garden, bringing a feeling of security and relaxation.

In China, when deciding where to build a new house, the feng shui master always would pose the question, 'Where are the nearest mountains and river?' The most auspicious place for any dwelling would ideally be a site with a river flowing in the front and mountains at the back. This shows the value placed by the Chinese on a human dwelling being 'held' by the energy of the landscape, and on free-flowing energy, in this case water. This 'holding' can be created even in a small city garden, not by mountains, but by the positioning of a good screening system of hedges or fences.

When planned with energy flow in mind, even a very small garden can feel spacious. You can achieve this by introducing meandering pathways and gently flowing water, and by enclosing the space with lush plantings, such as a shelter belt of graceful bamboos. These elements slow down and encircle the *chi* and allow visitors to slow down, too. They enable and encourage them to contemplate the beauty of the garden at a comfortable pace and to become relaxed and rejuvenated. The slowing down of movement, and thereby the mysterious slowing down of time, was commented upon by many a visitor who walked the pathways of The Feng Shui Garden at Hampton Court Palace Flower Show.

Near Toulouse, in southern France, I designed a garden for clients at their home called La Tanière, meaning 'animal's lair'. The house was situated in softly contoured and wooded land that could easily be imagined as one of Earth's safe havens. One of the clients, an acupuncturist who was familiar from his work with the Five Elements of feng shui, very much wanted representations of them to be included in the garden.

The position of an old well marked the focus of the design. From here, spiralling paths travelled out through the garden towards the new orchard and led to areas representing each of the Five Elements.

The Earth area overlooked the fields and took the form of a dry circle that contained rocks and a seat enclosed by a beech hedge. The Water circle consisted of a round pond with a fountain, to keep the water moving, and a small island that could be viewed from a seat; the whole area was richly and informally planted.

'Hot' colours and a fire pit were included in the Fire circle, while the use of metal arches and the wooded orchard completed the five elements of feng shui. A plan of La Tanière and more detailed information about the design and planting are given on page 47.

Above Chi is the Chinese word meaning life force or energy – 'Cosmic Breath' or 'Dragon's Breath'. The design and shape of these paths in The Feng Shui Garden are intended to slow down the flow of *chi*, just like the slowing of water movement in a meandering river.

Geopathic stress: modern-day energy mapping

'Geo', meaning earth, and 'pathos', meaning suffering, combine to indicate an intriguing sensory connection with the Earth. Geopathic stress is an ever-present phenomena below, above and on the surface of the Earth. It is a distortion, either man-made or natural, of the Earth's own natural electromagnetic field – its energy system.

Man-made disturbances could include such things as sewers and tall buildings, while natural disturbances could arise from deep underground water or changes in geological strata. The existence of ancient funeral pathways or connections between sacred sites can contribute to a particular energy signature. Where these have occurred, the gridwork of energy channels on the Earth's surface may start to conduct detrimental energy.

Whatever the reason, we know that Nature continuously demonstrates the urge to return to a state of balance and that facilitating this rebalancing can be a very important part of creating a sacred garden.

The study of geopathic stress, combined with a growing body of scientific research on electro-magnetic waves, unites the ancient art of dowsing with new research on the effects of the Earth's energy field on human beings, plants and animals. People living on a site of geopathic stress may experience continual tiredness, poor sleep patterns or a weakening of their immune system. Those people with health problems may experience a worsening of symptoms or a delay in recovery.

It seems that some individuals have a heightened sensitivity to the effects of electro-magnetic fields. These people would be more aware of artificially generated electro-magnetism from items such as mobile phones, electricity pylons and television satellite dishes.

In the garden, the influence of geopathic stress may have real consequences for sensitive people. For instance, placing a seating area for meditation

on an area of particularly strong geopathic stress may be distracting to our subtle sense of well-being and contemplation.

It is interesting to note that geopathic stress doesn't always have a negative effect in the garden. For instance, some plants, such as asparagus, oak trees, mushrooms and elderberry, are thought to thrive on it, while roses, azaleas, privet and celery seem to struggle.

Certain individuals are particularly sensitive to disruptions in the Earth's energy grid. People with this sensitivity are able to 'heal' such disruptions by carrying out energy-balancing techniques.

You may want to make use of this specialized information when trying to effect a subtle atmospheric shift in your garden. In fact, many feng shui practitioners use geopathic stress techniques in conjunction with their own traditional methods to achieve harmony.

Far left Giulia Dence, a geopathic stress consultant, dowses with a piece of freshly cut hazel. Hazel is a traditional country tool for dowsing and water divining and has been used for many centuries.

Left This copper coil is in fact one of the 'corrective' structures used in places of geopathic stress. Giulia recommended placing two of these at either end of the bamboo fence in my garden to shift the negative effects of crossing water lines. Placed against beach cobbles, it also acts as an attractive feature.

Energy in a hillside garden

A year after I first moved to my new home in Brownshill, Gloucestershire, England, I invited geopathic stress consultant, Giulia Dence, to take a look at the garden. Although it was coming along well, I had found that there were some areas that still didn't feel right.

After walking around the house and garden to gain an overall sense of the energies present – it's interesting to note that these energies are said to be up to 300–400 metres inside the earth – Giulia's first line of investigation was to survey the garden using her dowsing rods. She began by plotting the places where underground water was present. Later, when we were digging the soil, we discovered a pipe from the house to a known drain and this confirmed just how accurate the dowsing had been.

The garden was once a quarry and gradually, through digging to prepare beds, we had discovered a considerable amount of rubbish buried there, everything from old iron bedsteads to car petrol tanks. So as expected, Giulia discovered convoluted trackways of water travelling downhill and out of the garden.

There were complex lines of underground water terminating at a large beech tree and then travelling out of the garden on the east side. It is interesting that below this point of exit, the atmosphere in the garden seems to become more relaxed. In the areas where water was struggling to pass through, Giulia described a sense of energy 'turbulence' being amplified by, in this case, water flowing over an already disturbed area, in the form of buried rubbish.

I have now made this area under the beech tree into a naturalistic woodland garden, thereby allowing it to sit more comfortably in the surrounding woody environment. My gardener has dug up and disposed of a great deal of waste and replaced it with good soil and the lovely ground-cover plants have returned a new, healthy energy to this damaged piece of land.

My partner, James, had been urging me to place a seat in a particular position so we could take in the beautiful view of the valley, but something was keeping me from doing so. Giulia's dowsing showed that two underground water pathways crossed at exactly this spot, and such a configuration is known to bring an unsettled feeling. By adding metallic items, such as copper rods or a film of metal foil, the atmosphere will often improve. Giulia suggested two small copper coils be placed at either end of the nearby fence.

As the work in the garden proceeded, I felt easier creating a place to sit in the area where the water lines cross. Interestingly I chose to use Mediterranean plants and some metallic-coloured, silver-leaved plants, such as artemisia and lavender around a little circular lawn. Here we placed a timber seat, which feels just right and not uncomfortable at all – I'm sure Giulia's corrections have played their part in this happy resolution.

Giulia also highlighted other spots known as 'drains'. Drains are said to be the Earth's natural self-regulating system, but they can become blocked. Giulia uses a range of iron, magnetic or crystalline objects to either refract, absorb, deflect or block electromagnetic energy and to act as a corrective measure. Mysteriously, these solutions seem to enhance the energy in the troubled areas.

Right In the area in my garden where the two lines of underground water cross, I eventually placed a little circular lawn surrounded by shrubs, such as rosemary and cistus, herbaceous plants and ornamental grasses such as *Stipa tenuissima*. The bench, made from re-cycled teak, is now a lovely place to sit and view the valley below.

Far right A broad, steep set of steps lead to the lower, woodland area of my garden. This steep fall has been gently held back elsewhere by the placing of low trelliswork bamboo fences which prevent the feeling of 'falling', and separate the upper and lower gardens.
At the end of these steps are bamboo poles topped with lovely, smooth, large sea pebbles. The local limestone soil prevents camellias being grown here but by placing them in large metal containers (which also act as earthing factors) at the sides of the steps, I can create an unusual planting feature which slows down the journey along the steps.

Energy in a valley garden

A garden for which I have great fondness is situated in the valley below my garden. The whole area, known as the Golden Valley, is naturally beautiful, despite having an industrial past. Here, in this watery environment, specifically in the Valley of Seven Springs, is St Mary's Mill, originally the home and place of worship of the nuns of St Bridgit.

Ivy Cottage, a long, stone building encircled by ancient channels of water that flow both above and below ground, is part of the original mill complex – probably originally built for weavers. In summer, gentle swathes of herbaceous plantings border the lawn; there is also a small vegetable and herb plot. Next to an old mill wheel and flanked by the wood of St Mary's House, a seat has been placed where one can look back at the house and enjoy the sunshine.

Sculptor Alan Thornhill and his partner, Kate Shuckborough, have made their home here for the last five years. They have created this lovely garden partly as a place to display Alan's sculptures. I wanted to find out more about their relationship with the garden and the effect on them of so much water, so I invited Giulia to divine the water trackways using her dowsing rods.

Alan said that he felt he couldn't necessarily explain the effect that the water has had on their lives, but he has found it an extremely beautiful element, one that has inspired him in his work. Meanwhile, Kate said that, for her, the most exciting aspect of the garden's water was that it drew in all kinds of wildlife.

Immediately outside the kitchen windows is a fast-moving channel of water, which is directed underground into two man-made sluices and then disappears beneath the garden. Herons, dippers and ducks are frequent visitors, and kingfishers flash past the windows, bringing Alan and Kate great delight. In order to encourage further insect and animal visitors, Kate has added a circular pond, and this has introduced the contrasting quality of 'still' water.

Giulia dowsed the water flow and discovered that there were even more channels than Alan and Kate were aware of. In fact, the whole garden seems to be criss-crossed with underground water. It is possible that the area could have been a port at some time, like its sister mills in the valley, and Giulia's dowsing certainly suggested the presence of more open water in the past.

Another interesting observation was the placement of one of the larger bronze sculptures, entitled *Pygmalion*, between two channels of underground water. Alan and Kate chose the site so that the sculpture could be viewed from both the kitchen and the entrance to the garden, but is this piece of bronze preventing water from carrying energy away from the garden, in effect acting as an earthing rod? Perhaps this position was unconsciously chosen for its beneficial action on the site? We can only guess.

What is very clear is that the air in the garden at Ivy Cottage is full of the sound of water; in places, it even drowns out the sound of the road. It carries the natural beauty of wildlife, allows the musing of the artist and, I feel, creates an atmosphere of dreaminess at all times of the year.

Far left A little cascade
of water, typical of the
streams in the area around
St Mary's Mill.

Left Alan Thornhill's
sculpture, *Pygmalion*, in the
garden of Ivy Cottage may
be acting as an earthing
rod, as it has been placed
between two channels of
underground water. This
kind of unconscious placing
of features which act
effectively as 'corrections'
in a garden, often occurs
when the owners act
sensitively and intuitively to
the subtle energetic needs
of the land where they live.

Discovering your own garden's energy

The 'energy' we have discussed in this chapter can be most usefully understood, and felt, simply by being at peace in our garden space. Try sensing energy wherever you are, so that you are fine-tuning your sensitivities. When you return to your garden, be completely still. This will allow you to recall the feelings you have experienced and to tune in to your garden's unique energy signature.

In tracing the subtle forces in our gardens, it is easy to forget to add ourselves to the equation. Only by doing this can we work successfully with the atmosphere and spirit of our garden.

Profound information can come from time spent in stillness, when our natural gifts of intuition and creativity can readily emerge. These can offer important clues as to how to begin the task of designing our own soul sanctuary.

After periods of contemplation, it is valuable to ask yourself a range of questions before you begin to design. These questions will help determine where to place certain 'features'. I have found the following questions to be most productive.

How do I feel when I enter the garden?
How does my body feel here?
Where in the garden does my body feel best?
What does this garden contain that I love?
What would I like to feel more of?
What would I like to feel less of?
What would I most like to remove?
Is there enough light for me?
Is there enough shade?
Do I like the colours and textures?
Where do I feel most relaxed?
Where in the garden do I feel most like sitting or stopping?
What would make this space special for me?
What aspect of my life is uppermost in my mind when I am in this garden?
What natural element do I yearn for here?
What practical things do I need in the garden?
How do I feel when I leave?

By asking yourself these questions, you are recognizing the gifts of the garden and your own needs. If there are two or more people involved in the planning, it is helpful for each to spend time alone in the garden, going through the questions. Then, stroll around it together and share your feelings and desires for the proposed sanctuary. This gives a good foundation for the planning of the garden, and any overlaps or conflicting desires show up early in the process.

There may be areas that you feel should be left well alone and others that require balancing. Knowing when not to change something is important, too. It's worth spending as much time as possible getting this right at the start.

Before you begin to work out the details of your garden, it's a good idea to draw up a 'statement of intent'. I have often discovered that writing down what you want in a sacred space brings about a spontaneous change in its energy.

I would encourage all gardeners to acknowledge and include something of the wild places they have visited and to weave in the spirit of these places. Sometimes, it's hard to say what we want to include from our journeys; maybe just feelings or maybe something special, like a subtle new colour or the texture of a new plant.

Learning to dowse can be exciting, it can give you the confidence to acknowledge unseen energy in the garden, which you may have previously experienced only on an emotional level. Turn to page 154 for a guide to dowsing.

I always feel that the true test of how successful the energy work has been in a garden is to ask about the feelings experienced by the gardeners. Angie Avis, Broxmore Garden's organic vegetable grower, travels a long distance to work in the garden because she feels that, through handling the garden's soil, she receives what she refers to as the 'energy of the Earth'. She maintains that the spirit of the garden and its atmosphere keeps drawing her back.

Right To discover the energy in your own garden, move through the space slowly and silently, sitting occasionally and becoming aware of your own very personal feelings – remember that you and your energy are an important part of the garden. Explore even the smallest places; try sitting in different areas, right among the plants if you wish, observing scents and the movement of the air. These feelings need to be noted, they are part of the information that should be gathered before any careful designs or plans are created and they should form a guideline for future changes in the garden.

Following pages A view across the woodland area of my garden in Brownshill. A lovely piece of cut Cotswold stone, unearthed while preparing the soil, has been simply and beautifully sited by my partner, James. It marks the end of the wooded area and the beginning of a sunnier, open stretch of land. Uprights such as these help to 'hold' the garden both visually and energetically where land contours slope downward.

Universal symbols are present both in nature and in the creations of mankind. The web pattern, for example, is a symbol of the connectedness and the creativity of life. The sacred *Kalachakra* mandala in the Tibetan Peace Garden, London, has a mysterious quality, said to give its visitors an experience of the connectedness of all humans and their potential for peaceful co-existence.

Ancient symbols

Using ancient symbols

Discovering the mysteries of the symbols of the past is a visually exciting and spiritually stimulating approach to designing a garden. Symbols can cross the boundaries of language and can convey a deep wisdom beyond that of the spoken word. Ancient symbols can be seen as containing sacred information within 'shorthand' images – images that were designed for the contemplation of the viewer, who was not expected to be able to read, but who would be able to respond to the symbols in an intuitive way.

The mysterious beauty of symbols can please our aesthetic senses and satisfy us spiritually, even without a knowledge of their meanings. In his book *Spiral Patterns*, Aidan Meehan, an authority on Celtic art, comments that ancient symbols can provide a way of creating 'visual music' to replace storytelling.

Ancient symbols are potent containers of spiritual knowledge and are seen in both past and present spiritual systems. They are designed to transmit, mysteriously, the wisdom they carry in a visual form. Their attractiveness to the human soul was assured by their being created in diverse and personal ways by artists whose work was deeply connected to the social and spiritual worlds of their time.

Spiritual symbols are designed to invoke a strong emotional response, one that may even have a physical effect. We may be completely unaware of their power until that moment when we see and spontaneously respond to them. They make up a mysterious language that is sometimes available only to the initiated, being designed to ensure the secrecy and protection of sacred, arcane knowledge.

When we design our own sacred gardens, by including personally chosen symbols we can introduce the pictorial elements of our own spiritual language. Our own symbols may be expressed in our gardens, offering us the potential for their use as meditation tools.

The shapes of ancient maps of the universe, in the form of mandalas or labyrinths, can be formed in the garden in grass turfs, shaped paving or clipped plants, such as common box or cotton lavender. Overlaying these symbols on to a garden design, as demonstrated in various examples in this chapter, shows how creating them in the form of pathways and shapes on the ground enables them to be used as a visual or walking meditation.

Right across the world, people are drawing on ancient and modern symbols to express their own view of their inner world and of the universe that they live in. Sacred symbols and systems from across the globe, and from all creeds and cultural experiences, are bringing us the spiritual teachings we need to draw upon in a time described by the shaman and artist, Martín Prechtel, as one when our souls have become 'invisible'.

When asked what religion one should follow, the Dalai Lama, the spiritual head of Tibetan Buddhism, said that we should all look to the spiritual traditions of our homelands. Sensing the mysteries held in the places we make our home, choosing to draw on the symbols and traditions of our own native lands and then designing a personal, soulful garden can feel no less than creating a garden for the soul.

Far left The *Kalachakra* mandala, in London, England, is a beautiful example of an ancient symbol set in a contemporary garden. It is designed to invoke a shift in the consciousness of the viewer whereby they become increasingly aware of the vision held in the symbols of the mandala, one of a harmonious and enlightened world.

Left A spiral labyrinth garden, designed by Tom Stuart Smith for the Chelsea Flower Show, in London, England, captured the spirit and timeless design philosophy of the great garden designer André Le Notre. Between four and five thousand *Buxus sempervirens* plants were used to create these beautiful labyrinthine structures while centrally placed water fountains brought movement and life to its formality. Creating the effect of a medieval *mille fleurs* tapestry are two exquisitely planted lawns, scattered with buttercups and jonquils.

Spirals and labyrinths

We need to know certain things about sacred symbols in order to use them in our gardens. We need to learn about their shapes, colours and meanings, the plants and deities associated with them, and then we need to begin to explore what they may come to mean to us personally.

The earliest of symbols is the spiral, which is found all over the world, in cultures as diverse as Celtic, Hindu, Aboriginal and African. The spiral is said to be associated with the snake, a symbol of energy and of cyclic time. The upward and down-ward movement of the spiral may also represent the waxing and waning moon.

Spirals have been found on ancient pottery, surrounded by symbols of the year in which they were made. The archaeologist Marija Gimbutas describes ancient symbols in her book *The Language of the Goddess*. Marija is a world expert in the study of the prehistoric Goddess-worshipping cultures of ancient Europe. Observing the patterns of spirals on ancient pottery shards,

she comments that it seems as if the very power of the life force is represented in visual form.

Marija also illustrates another example of the use of the spiral, this time on megaliths. In Tarxien, Malta, the site of an ancient temple (c. early 3000BC), the spirals carved into megaliths can be seen to change into the shapes of plants, as leaves branch off from their ends.

She makes the point, too, that images of the Goddess on pottery often have spirals incised into their eyes. Marija says that this was done to energize the image, and not just for decoration, and that the spiral and snake symbols were inseparable from the Goddess: the coiling, skin-shedding, egg-laying serpent being the symbol of continuous movement and of the holding of energy to awaken dormant life power.

For Marija Gimbutas the vitality of the spiral as a symbol cannot be denied. She sees an inseparable association with what she calls 'serpent force' and the Goddess's energy.

Far left The seeds in the centre of the sunflower are a fine example of a spiral pattern formed in nature. Interestingly they also conform to the golden proportion (see page 82).

Left A simple and beautifully executed spiral in a tiny courtyard garden in Brighton, England, is made of slate and cobbles for a strong impact. Viewed from an upper window, the spiral draws attention to its centre.

More about spirals

Above The use of spirals in this traditional parterre garden in Jaarsveld, Holland, has a universal appeal – flowing continuous forms give the pleasure of movement in what would otherwise be a formal garden.

A natural, physical spiralling force is known to affect the germination and growth of trees and plants. Spiral growth can be seen in the formation of certain flowers, such as the datura and the sunflower, and in the fractal growth patterns in the natural world – from the formation of a cauliflower, to the wave patterns in the sea and satellite views of coastal patterns.

In an area of the Boyne Valley, in Ireland, at the megalithic tomb site of Newgrange, various spiral forms can be seen to have a fascinating depth of meaning. Aidan Meehan, who has studied these forms and the geometric way they can be created in his book *Spiral Patterns*, shows the versatile power of the symbol within modern design. At Newgrange, there is a very early labyrinth in the form of a double spiral. It is thought to represent going inwards into the small death and then going outwards to rebirth, into light and consciousness.

A spiral form of some kind included in an area of the spirit garden could represent a number of sacred themes, such as the movement of our consciousness within, the spiralling energy of *kundalini* – moving up from the base of the spine to the crown of the head, or a symbol of the life energy of the Goddess.

Spirals can be represented easily in the modern garden, as in the courtyard garden in Brighton on page 45, but they have also been a favoured form in the more traditional garden. The garden on the left, in Jaarsveld, Holland, uses clipped box hedging in the shape of spirals to create parterres for the enclosure of plants.

A spiral can be designed as a small, simple, freehand mark or as a meticulously calculated, geometric form, built on a grand scale. Spirals have, therefore, become a favoured and intriguing symbol, not just because of their ancient mystery, but also because they are easy to create.

The gardener wanting an easy way of producing a spiral can simply scratch the shape into the earth and then mark it out in stones. On the other hand, the mathematically precise designer can create plans following the instructions in Aidan Meehan's book. Here, the techniques for drawing spirals accurately are outlined step-by-step. Information is also given about the way such spirals have been used by carvers and craftspeople throughout the history of Celtic crafts.

In my garden design for La Tanière, in Southern France, a large garden area of over 30m (90ft) by 19m (60ft), I incorporated a triple spiral shape seen at Newgrange. At La Tanière, this spiral has been used to 'hold' areas representing the elements of earth, fire, air and water. As this was a large garden set in an even larger area of of woodland, a generously sized spiral form could be laid out on the ground as an important component of the design. Pathways have been designed to enable the visitor to walk this spiral shape.

Walking can bring a deeper and more meditative sense of the power of the spiral form, taking it firmly into the body. Plenty of time can be taken to move through this garden and feel the different qualities in the circular areas of the elements and spiralling movements of the paths.

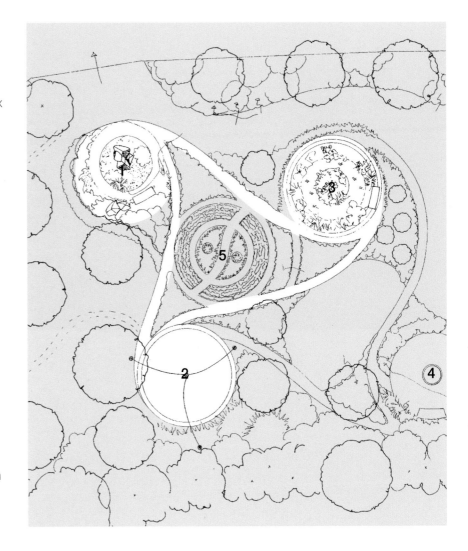

Above I have included the ancient triple spiral symbol in this garden design for La Tanière in southern France, as a representation of the ancient triple goddess; Maiden, Mother and Crone. The free-flowing, interlocking movement of the spiral blends beautifully into the surrounding landscape. The circular areas shown in this design each represent one of the elements of earth, fire, air and water.

1 The earth circle features a gravel path encircling a collection of pebbles, stones and crystals that represent the mineral worlds of the earth.
2 The air circle contains four upright poles that can hold swathes of light fabrics to blow in the breeze. Bamboos and grasses to bring the sound of the wind to life.
3 The water circle holds at its centre a small circular pond with a seat positioned close by to

enable the contemplation of the visiting wildlife.
4 The fire circle is surrounded by 'hot' coloured plants, such as *Crocosmia* 'Lucifer' and *Hemerocallis* 'Aztec'. It has a central fireplace and a surrounding semi-circular seat where a good-sized group of people can stare into the flames together.
5 The circular vegetable and herb garden benefits from its central position in the triple spiral.

Labyrinths

While the spiral is visually simple, the labyrinth is graphically complex. Labyrinths are said to represent the journey of the human soul on earth. The original purpose of the labyrinth was to provide a sacred pattern to be walked, to induce the shift in consciousness needed to bring about a certain inner transformation.

Labyrinths are found in many different forms, from primitive cave paintings to formal gardens. It is a fascinating thought that the classical labyrinth design appeared through history independently all over the world, in places as far apart as America, Australia and Europe. Labyrinths are distinct from mazes, which are a Victorian adaptation of the labyrinth, built for puzzlement and entertainment.

Recent studies suggest that the Italian painter, Sandro Botticelli (1445–1510), was inspired by the shape of an ancient Egyptian labyrinth. A similar labyrinth has been found in Jerusalem and is thought to have been used by early Christians.

The classical labyrinth, laid out according to a twelve-ring pattern and enclosing a meandering path, can be found in prehistoric, pagan carvings and also in later Christian churches. This is the pattern found on the floor of Chartres Cathedral, in northern France, which was built in 1230 and includes the now-famous 13m (39ft) diameter labyrinth, said to have the power to replenish and refresh the soul of the person walking its patterns.

Pilgrims travelled long distances to Chartres, entering via the Great West Door. They would walk shoeless up the nave and then begin to walk the flagstones of the labyrinth. On entering the central 'rose' – and standing upright and conscious of the building's sacred structure, geometry and beautiful rose window – the pilgrim was said to be able to stand perfectly aligned with the forces of earth and heaven and so able to receive great blessings.

We are experiencing a great renaissance of labyrinth-making in gardens and buildings. Old structures are being restored and new ones are being designed and built. Designer and builder Alex Champion loves to create labyrinths in his Californian landscape. One turf structure is sprinkled with daffodils in spring and is a modern version of the ancient Celtic maze. It has been created for the purposes of meditation.

Another labyrinth enthusiast is Jim Buchanan, a modern British labyrinth-maker who works with the resonances of his home landscape in Dumfries and Galloway, western Scotland. He isn't sure where his inspiration came from, although around the time he was born, his mother made a pottery pendant showing a labyrinth, which he later found.

Whatever his inspiration, Jim seems driven to keep making new labyrinths, usually on a large scale. He has made the largest permanent one in the world, at Tapton Park, in Derbyshire. This project reclaimed waste ground from a nearby building site, and the banks of the labyrinth were planted out with a variety of wild flowers.

A labyrinth made at his home looked and felt fully accepted into the landscape, even at its opening in the winter of 2000. No new materials were introduced into the landscape, but rather, existing ones were repositioned.

Above and right Two labyrinths by Jim Buchanan. The one above was made in the morning dew on the ground. The one on the right is in a clearing in the Galloway Forest near his home. It is a large-scale landform, made entirely from the earth dug at the site and designed to delight visitors as they come upon it in the forest.

Mandalas

A mandala is a symbolic, pictorial representation of the world and the universe, created by an artist with a spiritual intention. In Sanskrit, the word mandala means 'circle'.

An early mandala dates from around 25,000 years ago, in the form of a sun wheel carved into rocks. Mandalas are prominent in the ritual art of Tibetan Buddhism, where they are often found on sacred scrolls or as temple paintings. They can also be found in Hindu, shamanic and Aztec art, and in 21st-century contemporary art.

Many mandalas, particularly in Hindu and Buddhist traditions, follow a precise, symbolic format, with a series of interconnecting circles, squares and gateways that are embellished with dramatic, auspicious images and representations of the material and spiritual worlds.

The geometry of mandalas is usually like that of a wheel, with spokes connected to the centre, or axis. The centre represents the world axis, or the cosmic centre. Mandalas often display sacred geometry, the directions of the compass, significant colours and pictures of deities, animals and plants that evoke the spirituality of a particular culture.

To create a mandala is to produce a symbolic image of the beauty and mystery of the world. This can then be contemplated in meditation or used in ritualistic ceremony.

If you sit in the garden, on the ground, and mark out a space around you, you are defining yourself as being at the centre of the universe in your own mandala. You are beginning the act of creating a personal sacred space. To develop this mandala further, you might mark the eight points of the compass and represent the five elements of earth, fire, air, water and spirit. The mandala can be further decorated with significant, personal images, to build up a picture of the whole of your life at a given point in time.

The Swiss psychologist Carl Jung created mandalas with his patients as part of his psychotherapy practise. He brought mandalas to

wider attention and spoke of cultures that even used them to design whole cities. He pointed out that mandalas represent a picture of the wholeness of the psyche.

Creating a mandala in the garden is a wonderful way of expressing our own universe or personal truths, and observing the changes in a mandala's shape and colour as the seasons pass can deepen the dimensions of its form.

As far as design goes, a mandala can provide an excellent foundation for a garden plan. The geometric shapes within it are easily transferred on to a garden plot, whatever its size, and using whatever visual detail excites us or feels significant. Many of us have square or rectangular gardens, within which a circular mandala sits very well, made up of paths, hedges, flowerbeds or even water features.

Well-known examples of mandalas have been used by the world's religions. Christianity has the Rose Window at Chartres Cathedral, and Buddhism the *Kalachakra*, a mandala depicting the great Buddhist teaching of the Wheel of Time. Simply to gaze at the *Kalachakra* is said to invoke a vision of harmony and of an enlightened world.

A unique bronze cast of the *Kalachakra* is the focal centre of a most important 21st-century sacred garden, the Tibetan Peace Garden. Situated in Central London, the garden's design features the meeting of East and West and brings together images from traditional Buddhist culture

Right The *Kalachakra* mandala in the Tibetan Peace Garden; around it are placed stone seats for the visitor to sit and meditate upon its sacred message.

Far right This mandala design in the garden at Sticky Wicket in Dorset, England, was created intuitively rather than with precise geometric measurements. The garden features a sundial at its centre, a chamomile lawn and colour-themed beds. Self-seeded violas and cloud grass line the areas of chamomile and give the garden an unusual, ethereal quality.

and contemporary western art. It has been created as an affirmation of the wishes of the Dalai Lama and Buddhists all over the world for understanding and peace between cultures worldwide.

The garden design itself is a mandala of a Buddhist image known as The Wheel of Time. At its entrance is a stone pillar, the Language Pillar, on each side of which are carved messages from the Dalai Lama in English, Chinese and Hindi.

On the outer circle are four large stone sculptures, set on the polar axis, that represent the elements of earth, fire, air and water. A pergola planted with jasmine, honeysuckle and climbing roses links these stones. At the gateway to the inner mandala, the fifth element of space is represented by a single, circular stone. In Buddhism, these five elements make up the very nature of our existence on earth.

In the inner area, you can contemplate the spirit of the *Kalachakra* from any of the eight meditation seats. These are surrounded by plants and herbs from Tibet and from the Himalayas.

A medicine wheel garden

A client of mine in London, England, wished to create a sanctuary in her little courtyard garden, which could incorporate some of the indigenous North-American spiritual teachings that had recently influenced her. I suggested that a North-American medicine wheel could be laid out to provide her with a living representation of the teachings she loved.

The medicine wheel is the mandala-like sacred map that is used in various forms by the indigenous Indian tribespeoples of North America. The creation of a medicine wheel is, in itself, a sacred act and can therefore form part of a powerful journey of self-discovery, using the assistance of the ancestral traditions responsible for holding its mysteries.

Marks on the wheel spokes acknowledge the traditional eight compass directions: the cardinal points of north, south, east and west, and the non-cardinal points of south-east, south-west, north-west and north-east. Within the markings showing these directions as points on the spokes of the wheel, particular energies, it is said, can be invoked, or 'held', thereby 'activating' the wheel.

Top right The east point on the medicine wheel symbolizes a gateway through which energy or spirit enters a space. The element here is fire and the atmosphere would ideally be one of creativity and spontaneity. Lighting an evening collection of candles in the east place of the garden could mark an intention to bring fire into your life, maybe as a new idea or life situation.

Right The north is the place where the element of air is 'held' and here a set of bamboo wind chimes, hanging in the trees will symbolize this element.

The cardinal east point, for example, is said to be the place where Spirit will enter when called. The magical energy of fire resides here, and this is where the creative and magical 'east child' would sit in the circle.

In the same way, the north point would hold the element of air, the quality of the male deity and his associated animals, such as the eagle. The south point on the wheel is the place where the Goddess resides; the sacred world of the plants and the element of water. The west point usually holds the energy of Earth, her rocks, the soil and also, interestingly, the place of The Wise Inner Spiritual Guide.

Each North-American tribe created their own style of medicine wheel, with each direction having interesting differences, and yet similarities, of meaning. Slowly, the important, exciting and earthy teachings of the medicine wheel are being brought to us via teachers from North America, often in association with the shamanic path. The medicine wheel is a sacred focus for the shaman who is preparing for contact with the spirit world, and for healing rituals involving shamanic 'flight'.

The overlay of the medicine wheel on to this London garden brought an exciting design structure. It provided the chance to create various features and focal points, to represent each point on the wheel, and an opportunity to create a lovely place to sit in the sun and contemplate life.

On a deeper level, a medicine wheel in a garden gives the opportunity, as one walks from point to point, to meditate upon aspects of one's life. For example, visiting the east point in the garden may inspire the beginning of a new piece of work, or bring an insight into why spontaneity is missing in our lives.

The totality of the medicine wheel brings a sense of the 'wholeness' of one's life by bringing together all the aspects of personal life through its expressive illustration.

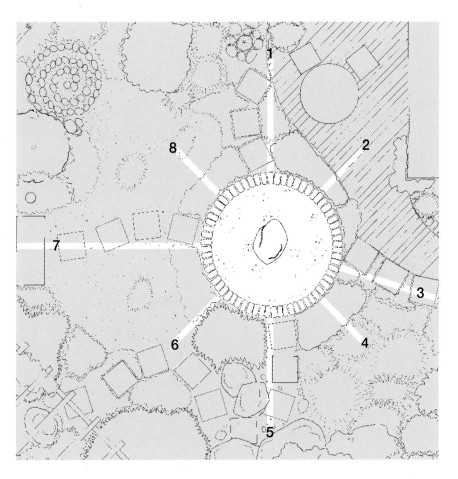

Above This is the garden design for a medicine wheel courtyard garden in London. The four cardinal points are marked by curving paths moving out from the centre circle. The non-cardinal points are also represented, by the cobble spiral symbolizing Design of Energy in the north-east, for example. Here a mirror is hung on the wall which will reflect the spiral and yourself. Your body movement will be seen giving information about the state of your own energy at that moment and an invitation to consider the spiralling energy of nature.

1 The east, where Spirit enters the wheel. Fire is represented here in the form of candles.
2 The south-east, the place of the Ancestors and Self Concept.
3 The south, the place of the Goddess and the Feminine, the Sacred Plants and the element of water
4 The south-west, the place of The Dream.
5 The west, the place of the Inner Teacher and the element of earth.
6 The north-west, the place of Karma and our Book of Life.
7 The north, the place of the God, the Masculine and the Sacred Animals and the element of air.
8 The north-east, the place of Design of Energy.

The East Garden

Right When designing the East Garden I wanted to design simply and include a range of ancient shamanic symbols close to Dawn's heart. Looking at this overlay we can see clearly the shape of a serpent. The circular pattern at the entrance gateway (the bottom of the plan), marks a place of stillness where the person considers entering the garden through the 'virtual' fence. Paths lead to the mirrored bowls of Narcissus for staring into and contemplating the ego; on to the central medicine wheel, water snake and fire moon; on to the old tree stump; on further to a statue of Athena and the meditation house.

1 The full moon, represented by an underlit disc of onyx.
2 and 3 The waxing and waning moon, represented by two steel containers, one for water and one for fire.
4 The entrance of the garden and the marked place where spirit enters the ground.
5 The place where the statue of Athena is positioned and surrounded with ornamental grasses.
6 A snake sculpture water feature, mounted on the wall and feeding water into the water moon.
7 A large tree stump, a place to sit and view the fire moon when it's lit and to muse underneath the big trees of the garden.
8 Meditation House under the Copper Beech tree.

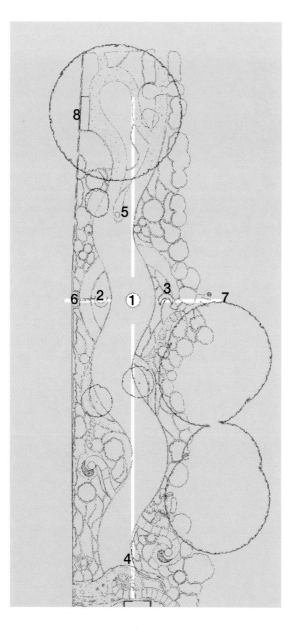

Dawn McConnell's brief for her garden design included the wish to combine both Buddhist and shamanic teachings in a way that would create a garden for use in her psychotherapy work and as her own retreat from her busy family life. The East Garden, at East Dean House, in Hampshire, England, needed to represent these aspects in a very subtle way and on a far larger scale than that used in the London medicine wheel garden.

Dawn wanted the garden, at first sight, to seem simply a well-designed and beautiful space with a sense of mystery. The deeper meaning and symbology was to be revealed slowly, only by spending contemplative time there.

This subtlety was partly effected by designing the planting in a traditional way. Particularly, the new garden would provide a beautiful view of a classic English herbaceous border, especially from the upper windows of the house, which overlooked the garden.

Dawn has a passionate interest in the way that magical symbols from all around the world share common threads. When we first surveyed the site, checking the polar compass directions, Dawn asked me to overlay the ancient, sacred, North-American medicine wheel map and to consider the Chinese directional system.

After many years studying and practising Buddhist teachings, Dawn began to draw also from shamanic teachings, which are particularly valuable in her current work as a psychotherapist. In designing the East Garden, together with taking into consideration the very practical aspects of soil type and the sun/shade question, the inclusion of an overlay and an intention of sacredness in the form of the medicine wheel brought an exciting edge to my work.

The garden is a long stretch of lawn, bounded by an old, tall brick wall on the south side and a beautiful boundary of trees on the north side. The entrance is on the east side, adjacent to the house, and at the west stands a giant copper beech. After considerable soul searching, I drew a bold, sinuous, meandering serpentine shape through the garden, from the entrance to the tree, since the snake is an significant shamanic animal and symbol to Dawn.

The entrance to the garden begins with steps leading to a spiral brickwork and paved area with a central mosaic. A simple, cast-iron fence gives the illusion of being continuous, but on close

examination is quite 'open'. This adds the sense of illusion that is important to Dawn, and which is an element of both Buddhist teachings and shamanic experiences.

At the centre of the garden, sitting directly on the earth, was placed a simple, circular disc of milky-white onyx. It is gently lit underneath and represents the full moon. At the south side of the circle, a container, in the form of a new crescent moon, receives water that falls from a wall-mounted serpent feature. At the north side, a container shaped like an old crescent moon, can be used to hold a fire, and is designed for use in night-time ceremony.

At the west end of the garden is a beautifully crafted Meditation House, its design inspired by Japanese architecture. Its purpose is to provide contact with the varying seasonal elements in the garden while, if necessary, protecting the user from the rain. It has become the place Dawn completely escapes to; on warm summer nights she can even sleep there.

The focal point of the garden, at the end of the serpentine walk, is a specially commissioned sculpture, created by sculptress Janis Ridley. It is of the goddess Athena, who is surrounded by plantings of ornamental grasses. This gives her a airy feel, air being the element most closely associated with the qualities of Athena. She is shown walking together with her handmaiden (Shame), a figure of great importance to Dawn in her psychotherapy work with her clients.

Interestingly, Dawn asked a local dowser to check the energy lines of the garden after the design had been completed. He noted particularly the correct position of the central moon and found a place just outside the garden gates that Dawn has chosen to mark as the point of the entrance of spirit into the ground. This spot is marked by a funnel-shaped opening in the ground, covered by a lid that has Dawn's personal sacred symbols engraved upon it.

Previous page top Ground cover planting at East Dean House, including *Erythronium revolutum* and *Viola glabella*.
Below The lovely foliage of *Adiantum pedatum* and *Pleioblastus viridistriatus* bring brightness to the shady places underneath the trees.

Top right The hand-crafted Japanese-style, oak Meditation House seen nestling under the copper beech as its leaves begin to turn to autumn gold. Here is a space for Dawn to escape and meditate, dream or even sleep on a warm night.

Below right The stainless steel Fire Moon lit for an evening celebration. On the other side of the garden is a second moon which contains water flowing from the wall-mounted snake water feature.

Far right A dense carpet of ground cover plants; *Lamium maculatum* 'Beacon Silver', *Ajugareptans* 'Catlin's Giant' and the leaves of *Geranium pratense*, growing under a copper beech tree.

Feng shui and the ba gua

The ancient system of feng shui is of particular interest today and is one of the ways in which modern people are learning the subtleties and benefits of 'energy' management. A full study of feng shui and how it can be used in a garden space is extensive, but there are several guiding points that can be noted by anyone wanting to design with these ancient principles in mind. *Chi* is said to be the movement of life energy, and keeping this flowing rather than static is important to our health, emotional well-being, wealth and even spiritual development.

The elements of earth, water, metal, wood and fire should be represented in the garden. The use of organic methods should also be considered, and possibly planting by the movements of the moon, or even the planets. Together, these will help to achieve the desired result – a harmonious garden space that will mirror a balanced natural world.

I have found that by using the ancient, nine-square, *ba gua* grid as a template, a garden can be created that takes into account the most important factors of feng shui. The *ba gua* not only helps to create harmony and the flow of *chi*, but can also help us to express in our garden what we wish to bring into our lives.

At the centre of the grid is the *tai chi* 'void', said to be the place of complete harmony and balance. Around this are eight areas that pertain to different aspects of life. They resonate with particular colours, compass directions and one of each of the fundamental elements of earth, fire, water, wood and metal.

This eight-sided, geometric shape can be more usefully understood in terms of designing outdoor spaces if we see it as a more organic shape, like a spider's web. This illustrates the need to stay flexible when using any ancient system. I am personally rather averse to seeing straight lines of demarcation between features in a garden; I prefer a gentle merging of different areas, one into another.

A Moroccan-style garden using feng shui

Debbie Carslaw's garden can be viewed from the balcony and upper windows of her house and is a leafy, tucked-away spot in a busy area of London. She asked me to help her to create a fruit and flower-filled sanctuary garden, inspired by the art of Morocco. As a design tool, I used the principles of feng shui, and overlaid the nine-square grid of the *ba gua* on to a Moroccan-influenced design.

A new garden is a wonderful opportunity to clear unwanted clutter and make a fresh start. This is always good, whether indoors or out, and is highly recommend by feng shui practitioners as a way to allow room for the *chi* to move freely.

When designing a garden, the *ba gua* needs to be positioned so that any of the three 'gates of *chi*' are placed over the entrance to it. Here the entrance was via the kitchen door in the north.

The journey of life starts at this point, as the *ba gua* identifies this area as that of your Life's True Journey, popularly known as the place of your career. The colours to be shown are black and blue and the element is water. To begin the Moroccan theme, blue and white floor tiles were laid in this part of the garden in a striking, traditional Moorish pattern. A water feature couldn't be placed just outside the door, so a wall-mounted, blue, trickling, water bowl was positioned above two mosaic-tiled tanks containing water lilies.

From here, the *chi* moves anti-clockwise to the place of Mentors in the north-west. The element of metal was represented by silver-leaved plants such as lavender and helianthimums cistus.

In the Chinese system of feng shui, the west is the place of the element of metal, children, creativity and new projects. Here, I placed a cast-iron seat so Debbie could take time to consider her own creativity. A kiwi fruit and gooseberries in pots were also placed here.

In the south-west, the place of marriage and relationships, I included a statue of two figures

Far right top Debbie Carslaw's Moroccan-style garden was designed using feng shui principles. In the centre is this little splashing water feature surrounded by blue tiles. Overhanging palms and fig leaves provide a North African atmosphere.

Below A garden with Moroccan-style features was created with an overlay of the nine-section *ba gua* grid. This brought a lovely flowing pathway through the garden, leading seamlessly from one area to another. Fruits, flowers and herbs were blended as would be a Moroccan courtyard and the life aspects of the *ba gua* were subtly represented in various design features.

1 North, the place of our Life's True Journey, sometimes called the place of our Career.
2 North-west, the place of Networking and Mentors, often called helpful people.
3 West, the place of Children and Creativity.
4 South-west, the place of Relationships, Marriage and Romance.
5 South, the place of Personal Recognition, often called Fame.
6 South-east, the place of Wealth and Prosperity.
7 East, the place of Elders, Teachers, Family and Health.
8 North-east, the place of Contemplation, Stillness and Knowledge.
9 The *tai çhi* void, an area of simplicity and Unity – to me the area most suited to a naturalistic look. The meandering path is simply flanked with herbs and shrubs.

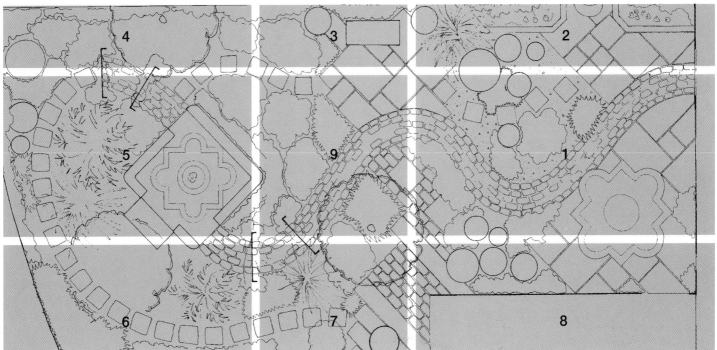

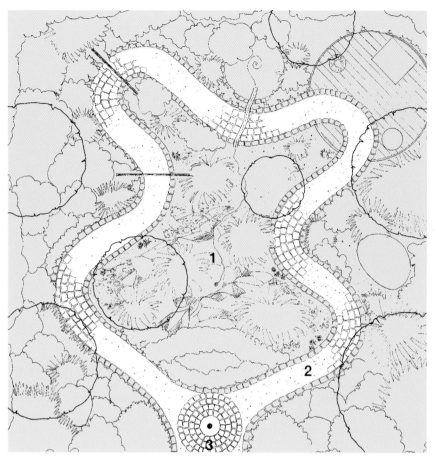

Above This garden design for The Feng Shui Garden at Hampton Court Palace Flower Show, 1999, shows the predominant and yet subtly disguised shape of the ancient goddess designs found on pre-historic European pottery. Within this 'body' is held a representation of a wild place in nature.

1 The *tai chi* centre of the garden, the place of the void, represented by a garden of grasses, rocks and pebbles and a spring gushing through the rocks.
2 The meandering path forming the ancient shape of the body of the Goddess and also allowing free movement of *chi* in the garden.
3 The entrance to the garden where the Moon Gate was positioned (see page 28).

surrounded by the associated colours of yellow in the euphorbia and the rose, 'Gloire de Dijon'.

Moving to the place of Fame, or Personal Recognition, in the south, I planted tall, red dahlias to introduce firey tones into this area. In the place of Wealth and Prosperity, the south-east, I placed bamboo and a fig to represent fruiting prosperity.

Moving to the east place, a mature bay tree was retained to represent wood in the place of Elders and Teachers. The colour green was shown by the grouping of evergreen shrubs such as camellias and a phormium.

On finally reaching the north-east zone, one finds the place of Contemplation and Stillness. This is akin to the element of earth, and to colours such as browns and beiges. Here, an open area of earth and large terracotta pots represented these factors. Space was left for a seat to offer the possibility for stillness.

The *tai chi* centre had to be moved south as the garden is a slight L-shape. It was created as a typical Moorish-shaped and tiled peaceful seating centre, through which the path entered and left.

The Goddess at Hampton Court

Another garden in which I used feng shui for guidance in the design was The Feng Shui Garden for the Hampton Court Palace Flower Show in 1999. Some interesting original aspects of the Chinese tradition arose during its creation.

A beautiful, hand-crafted, green-oak moon gate stood at the entrance to the garden. I placed this in the unconventional, and yet to me appropriate, south gate. Sometimes you have to break the rules of ancient systems in the name of beauty, and maybe even to just please yourself.

It was a Chinese visitor who encouraged me to speak of the 'story' of the garden – how it was that the idea for the garden actually came about, or might have arisen from a wild place somewhere in nature. In describing this to him, I found myself sharing this information for the first time.

The *tai chi* centre of this garden was, in fact, a representation of the wild source of the garden. Here, a flowing spring would have burst through the ground and travelled to the north point of the garden. The spring and stream were surrounded by natural grasses and pebbles, thereby representing this wilderness.

The centre was further surrounded by the meandering pathway, which I drew quite spontaneously in the design stages, in the ancient shape of the body of the Goddess. Around here, and marking the perimeter and all the other associated *ba gua* zones, were placed the cultivated plants in her honour.

Top right The central area of large stones and grasses represents what is known as the *tai chi* void. I chose to make a naturalistic centre of rocks and flowing water among the grasses and only added a sprinkling of flowers – something more akin to the natural landscape from which the garden sprang.

Below right The circular pond is fed from water flowing from the spring in the *tai chi* centre. The sculpture appears to be diving into the water and is surrounded by plants such as lavender and salvias, whose blue flowers are representative of the colours associated with this part of the *ba gua* grid.

The Qabala and designing with the tree of life

Above An ancient oak tree is growing in Windsor Great Park, Berkshire, England. Contemplating the image and energy of such a grandfather tree makes a wonderful meditation before beginning the exploration of the ancient study of the Qabala or Tree of Life.

Right In the Quabala garden the very mysterious and feminine power zone or *sephira* of Darth is associated with the element of water and the High Priestess of the Tarot. Her colours are blues, blacks, and silvers, represented here in the delicate flowers of *Campanula rotundifolia*, the purple flowers of *Penstemon* 'Papal Purple', the metallic foliage of the fern *Athyrium otophorum* var. *okanum* and the black leaves of *Ophiopogon planiscapus* 'Nigrescens'. Centrally placed in a bowl of water, pebbles and stones is a ball of black obsidian.

Another fascinating example of an ancient map of 'inner space' is the Judaic tree of life, otherwise known as the Qabala. The tree of life is said to illustrate the passage of spiritual life being travelled by an initiate wishing to become 'Godlike'. It charts a journey through the darkest material realms of the soul towards the highest places of illumination.

The Qabala enjoyed a great revival of interest at the turn of the 19th century. At this time, the Western esoteric arts were being reclaimed, partly as a result of disillusionment with the Christian church's inability to provide a full picture of the universe at a time when the scientific world was revealing the true age of the Earth.

The Qabala contains ancient Jewish esoteric wisdom, held within a tree-like map on whose branches are held *sephira*. These are described as being 'power' zones that describe landmarks on the journey of the soul. Each of the different *sephira* has positive and negative qualities, correspondences with certain gods, goddesses and archetypes and associations with particular elements, colours, planets and human characteristics.

The study of the *sephira* and their continued contemplation can bring about a developing consciousness through different areas of the self, the psyche and the spirit. This growth leads to an increasing awareness of the inner self, essential in order to climb the tree-like ladder of mystical ascent.

The symbolic tree is likened to an actual living tree that can 'grow' within us as we evolve spiritually. Rather than abandoning the lower *sephira* or self as we grow, through the study of the Qabala, we can learn to integrate all the aspects of ourselves and hence move towards what Jung called 'individuation'.

A few years ago, I was fortunate enough to be asked to design a garden for a practising qabalist in southern England. Her garden surrounded her single-storey home, and although gardening had long been a favourite pastime of hers, she was perplexed about how to include successfully some of the complex symbology of her own spiritual practice.

By overlaying the Qabalistic tree of life on the map of the client's house and garden, I was able to create a simple garden design with distinct areas to represent the individual *sephiras*. I chose to express these mostly by using the colours associated with the *sephiras* and by designing creatively with plants whose leaves, flowers or berries could serve to make such colour statements.

The zone Tiphareth, representing the sun, which, because of its central place on the tree, needed to be positioned in the house in order to

Right The Qabala is overlaid on a garden design for a practising qabalist. The central rectangle is the house. There are plants that resonate with the different *sephiras*, or zones, and plants whose energies relate to the nature of those places. I placed plants and features which represent these qualities, thereby bringing the Tree of Life out of the text book and into the living world.

1 Kether, the zone of the Self, the planet Neptune and the plants almond and chamomile.
2 Chokmah, the zone of spiritual will and wisdom and the plants frankincense and rosemary.
3 Binah, the zone of understanding and spiritual love, the planet Saturn, and the plants myrrh and comfrey.
4 Chesed, the zone of love and mercy, the planet Jupiter and the plants cedar and borage.
5 Geburah, the zone of will and severity, the planet Mars and the plants cypress and borage.
6 Tiphareth the zone of beauty and transformation, the sun and the plants hawthorn and the rose.
7 Netzach, the zone of feelings, the planet Venus and the plant verbena.
8 Hod, the zone of thoughts and the planet Mercury and the herbs rosemary and sage.
9 Yesod, the zone of the subconscious, the Moon and the plant lavender.
10 Malkuth, the zone of the physical body and the earth, associated with sandalwood and meadowsweet.
11 Daath, the zone of knowledge, the planet Pluto and the herbs Balm of Gilead and eucalyptus.

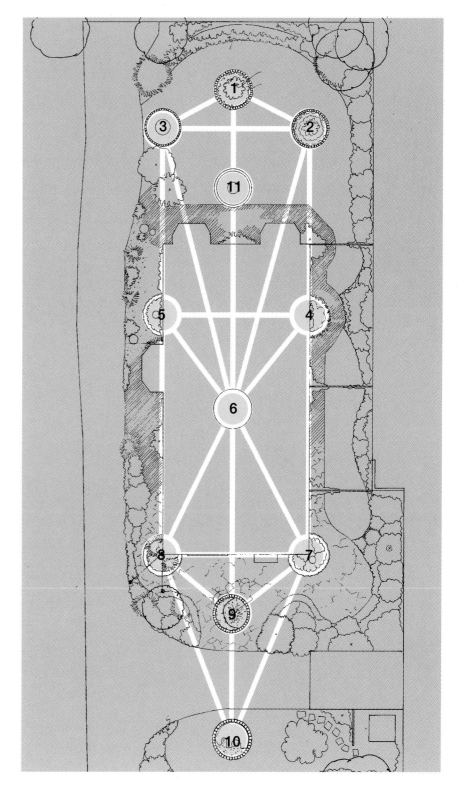

conform to the plan, happened to fall in the spot in the house where the altar is placed. All the other zones were represented in the garden as circular areas containing different plantings and features.

The zone Malkuth is associated with the earth and living things, and all inward journeys start here. At this spot, I added the client's favourite North-American animal symbol, the bear, which is also associated with the element of earth. By using common box, clipped to a bear-like shape and surrounded by brown-coloured pebbles, a simple, strong symbol was created. This felt appropriate to represent the beginning of the journey.

I chose the zone of Yesod, the area associated with the moon, as the spot for a splashing fountain and a moon-shaped symbol formed from clipped teucrium plants.

The *sephira* of Netzach, the area which is associated with Venus and earthly love, seemed to me to be the perfect place for the inclusion of the scented lily, *Lilium regale*, of romantic, heady-scented roses, such as 'Guinée' and 'Heritage', and the soft flowers and foliage of verbenas and spiraea.

A more tricky zone to define was the opposing area of Hod, which represents the intellect and rational thinking. Here, I drew on the associated colour of orange and included architectural plants, such as dog-lily varieties and red-hot pokers, shaded by an elegant golden *Gleditsia* tree.

The zone of Darth, the watery, mysterious sephira of the High Priestess, was represented by dark, shiny pebbles and obsidian, planted around with black iris and lilyturf 'Nigrecens'.

The zone of Kether symbolizes the dawning of creation, and here I placed white lavender and roses. In the borders beyond, I placed silver birch, bamboo and white 'Iceberg' roses, to create the ethereal quality of the Limitless Light beyond.

Preparing a garden design using this ancient and complex system was an exciting process,

which demanded that I take a considerable amount of time, commitment and a personal contemplation of the Qabala.

Each zone took a lengthy time to design, even though the resulting garden plan seemed relatively simple. Creating a sacred garden using such powerful ancient symbols will certainly affect the life of anyone involved in the making of it, from the client to the designer, the builders and gardeners.

Six years on from her garden's beginning, Katherine says that although the presence of the symbols of the Qabala are known to her, they are very discreet. The garden they are set within has been completely transformed, due partly to the recommended removal of a row of *Leylandii* trees and the resultant increase in light.

Again, the combination of practical and inspirational elements in a design have brought about the transformation of a space. The alchemists referred to the Tree of Life as the Tree of the Philosophers; Jung called the process of growing this tree within ourselves, 'Active Imagination'. Placing this ancient map in a garden brings the tree alive and thus constantly present in our lives, ready for its contemplation.

Right The *sephira* of Malkuth is said to resonate with the element of earth, so I have placed here two mysterious pieces of tree root, shaped like a dragon and a snake, which I discovered fallen onto a beach in Devon from eroding cliffs above. Bronze *Carex comans*, the dark leaves of violas and the autumn leaves of *Azalea luteum* in a large terracotta urn, all add to the earthy qualities of this zone.

Zodiac and the Tarot

The ancient signs of the zodiac are symbols whose meanings are illustrated in the stars. This ancient science of the interrelationships between planets, stars and the Earth developed when people considered the Earth to be a mirror of the heavens. Hence the expression 'As above, so below'. Astrology combines the study of the stars and the philosophy of interconnectedness between the cosmos and the individual self.

At night, we can see, even if we don't know their meanings or patterns, the stars of the zodiac, varying by season and hemisphere, shining above our gardens. Again, as with other ancient symbols, the signs of the stars tell stories without words. They come from an age when few people could read, but they were more likely to be able to decipher visual images intuitively. Now of course, the reverse is probably true.

In Broxmore gardens, Hampshire, there is a beautiful, specially commissioned, tiled floor. This was created for the circular meditation arbour at the centre of the garden and features the signs of the zodiac. The visitor can enter and take a seat next to any sign they wish and contemplate their connection to it, surrounded by the perfumes of the climbing roses and the traditional Maryan plants, sacred to the Virgin Mary, growing in the walls of the arbour. These include bellflowers, lilies and lady's mantle.

One way to bring the big story of the stars down into our gardens is to focus on our own personal star sign and to create ways to express its qualities in our garden. My star sign, Scorpio, is said to be characterized by the colours of scarlet, dark red and black. Its symbol is a scorpion, and its stinging tail and its habit of carrying its offspring on its back tells of its nature; despite being able to sting when attacked, it guards a deep and sensitive inner nature.

Some of my personal favourite flowers tend to be those whose colours are deep reds, strong scarlets and even blacks. In the Cotswold stone-edged beds at the entrance area of my garden, I have used a deep purple Japanese maple, together with half-standard 'Deep Secret' roses, chocolate cosmos, the cinquefoil 'Gibsons Scarlet', bugbane, dahlia 'Bishop of Llandaff' and the deepest dark-red cactus-flower dahlias.

I have lightened this deep gathering of beauties by adding the leaf interest of the Chinese sacred bamboo, with its green and reddish tints, and a climbing rose, 'Mme Alfred Carrière', which weaves though the back-wall planting of honey-suckle and flowers intermittently in this late-flowering scheme. Edge plantings of deep blue/purple-flowering hyssop, background plantings of windflowers and magenta cactus-flower dahlias add a sparkle of light in the depths of red.

This planting reigns from the end of August until my October birthday, when the Japanese maple loses its leaves and the dahlias retreat as the frosts advance. The death and decay of life is as important – particularly to a Scorpio – as the glorious, blooming phase of life, and the whole ritualistic process of lifting and storing the dahlia corms for overwintering until replanting in the spring, brings further meaning.

The Tarot may be as ancient as the science of astrology. No one really knows, although it is thought to have arrived across Europe from the Far East via gypsy travels. The story goes something like this. When the ancients were trying to decide how best to ensure that their wisdom would survive, they had to choose between a book and a game. A game was chosen, as it was felt that humans were far more likely to remain interested in something that was fun.

The Tarot contains all the 'big' stories of the nature of humanity in the form of a kind of game, with the major characters having archetypal meanings. The cards are used for divining the future and are, in fact, the precursors of modern-day playing cards.

Like astrology, the Tarot offers a rich sense of interconnectedness between ourselves, nature, the four elements of earth, fire, air and water, and the great, age-old stories and characters that abound in myth and magic. Laid out as a circular spread of cards, the story of the Tarot follows the classical 'Fools Journey', in the form of a mandala that has no beginning and no end.

A striking example of a garden designed to display the main characters, or major arcana as they are known, is one found in Tuscany, in Italy, where an on-going project by artist Niki de Saint Phalle involves the creation of a Tarot garden in the style known popularly as 'outsider art'. Her style is said to have been influenced by the Spanish artist, sculptor and graphic artist Pablo Picasso (1881–1973), the Spanish architect Antonio Gaudi (1853–1926) and the French painter and sculptor Henri Matisse (1869–1954).

Slowly, Niki is creating giant structures that can be entered, as if they were multicoloured grottoes. They are built to give the visitor a direct experience of the archetypal energy of the Tarot cards, using ones such as The Tower, The High Priestess and The Magician.

Left The tulip 'Black Parrot', with its deepest, darkest red petals, is perfect to represent the qualities of Scorpio in the spring. Later in the year plants such as *Cimicifuga* var. *cordifolia* 'purpurea', the deep red rose 'Deep Secret', the turning and brightening autumn leaves of *Acer palmatum* 'Atropurpureum' and the brighter red flowers of the dahlia 'Bishop of Llandaff' will all flower until October or November, even defying the first frosts.

Living and designing with ancient symbols

Creating gardens that include ancient symbols brings the opportunity to uncover the deeper, spiritual meanings that were important to our ancestors, and to rediscover their significance for today's world. Rather than learning about them in a dry, intellectual fashion, by making them real and placing them on the ground we walk on, they are injected with life and their meanings opened up.

Living and working with such symbols in the form of growing plants can bring a gradual unfolding of their meanings. We might make a space in the garden where we can rake a spiral in gravel, or use annual bedding plants to create an astrological symbol that we will see just for the summer; the next year we can create something new, and so on.

This experimentation will further encourage the exciting creation of our own new symbols and the reworking of old ones. Making mandalas for instance, can become a never-ending passion, wherever we find ourselves, whether on the beach, in woodland or garden, and with stones, sand, earth or plants.

Whether we create the symbols subtly or in outrageous statements, the choice is ours. As with all garden designs, everything is determined by the gardener's tastes and preferences. Remember, we don't need to make a Chinese- or Japanese-style garden because we are experimenting with feng shui; think of the Moroccan garden on page 58.

Such an approach is an excellent way to further private ideas that are dear to you. In a similar vein, my Feng Shui Garden at the Hampton Court Palace Flower Show was designed to retain a mystery – I deliberately hid away the body of the Goddess within the pattern of the meandering paths of the garden. I kept this secret, safe from the busy world of the Hampton Court Press, whom I didn't feel would be receptive to the idea. It was a secret overlay of an ancient and sacred shape and symbol, known by the few, but kept safe from the many.

Right At Parham Park, West Sussex, England, Adrian Fisher has made a contemporary maze in an area of perfectly flat grass surrounded by mature trees and hedges. In the early morning heavy dew accentuates the form of the maze, which has been created in a loose freehand way. Walking the lines brings a freer feeling of flowing movement, rather than one of being directed, as in a more formal maze.

Universal patterns

From the spiral pattern held in the centre of a growing flower to the image of a far-distant spiral galaxy, the universe develops in magnificent and sacred patterns.

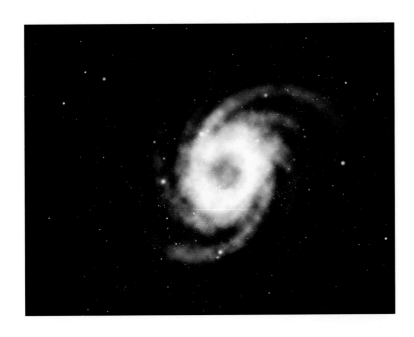

Seeing universal patterns

Becoming aware of the ever-present and ever-changing forms in nature and in the cosmos, both visible and invisible, can accelerate a realization that the earth upon which our own gardens are growing is a microcosm of the whole, much wider universe.

In this chapter I want to focus on the universe itself as a subject from which we can draw inspiration for the design of our landscapes, and on how reflecting the truths of the universe can be part of a spiritual direction in the work of the garden designer.

We live in a spiral galaxy and a picture of such a galaxy, like the one on page 71, shows the shape of one of the most ancient symbols, the spiral, which we can see in repeated again and again all manner of human art-making.

The cosmos is, of course, the big picture for us, and cosmological forms have always been a powerful source of inspiration for designers and artists from ancient times to the modern-day era. Through these cosmological forms we can begin to experience our own inner landscapes and understand how they relate to the universal stories and patterns.

When we look carefully we can see that there are identical patterns forming in both the macro world of space and the micro worlds of life on our planet. As intuitive human beings we are often mysteriously drawn to reflect these patterns in our work and we find them both aesthetically and spiritually satisfying, whether or not we understand their origins.

A study of universal symbols is a journey through space and time, and includes a look at the ancient and modern uses of sacred geometry and the new geometry seen in fractal images. In this chapter I want to explore the way in which the past creators of landscapes and buildings have included cosmic information in many of their creations and how designers today are still using the same principles.

Left and right A Zen garden in Blockley, Gloucestershire, England, and the sun setting at Worms Head in Wales. The light-path of the sun is echoed in the line of paving in the Zen garden; the ripples of the sea are represented in the raked lines in the gravel, and the island of planting is like the island in the sea. In such ways nature is reproduced in man's own creations.

Temples

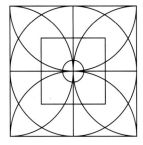

People of ancient times were frequently influenced by the cosmos in the designing and building of their temples, and these influences can also be useful when we are thinking about our own sacred garden spaces.

The structures of temples were designed to represent the position of humanity in relation to the universe, indeed to be a reflection of it. At the very centre of the sacred place was always placed the human psyche.

The human body itself was often thought to be a reflection of the cosmological order. Ancient tombs were often constructed in the shape of the human body with an inner space shaped like a womb, where the corpse itself was interred, enabling a symbolic re-birth to take place.

The Egyptians believed that the universe was our 'Great Dwelling', the place from where we came and where we wished one day to return. The body of the Goddess Nuit was perceived as being the night sky itself – the cosmos across which the moon, stars and planets could be seen to sail.

Images of Nuit's curving body studded with stars can be found in countless Egyptian tombs, she was seen as the cosmos itself, holding within her all the mysterious worlds of the gods beyond the earthly plane.

The hindu Vedas contemplated the structure of the universe in beautiful poetry, they saw the universe as being spherical. Therefore, creating a spherical space was thought to encourage visits from gods and the spirits, as they would feel at home in a structure with this form.

The ruined Mexican city of Chichén Itzá on the Yucatan Peninsula was built by the Maya (c600–830AD) and is one of the best examples of astronomical sacred architecture. Within it lies the Caracol observatory, oriented to the rise and fall of the Morning Star, sunrise at midsummer and midwinter, and the setting of the Pleiades.

Sightings of stars were made by eye through slits in the walls enabling the Mayans to collect data on their sacred planet Venus (The Morning Star) and to develop extremely accurate predictions of its path through the sky.

In the circular earth lodges of the Pawnee North American tribes, the cardinal compass directions are used to design the structure and sacred interior layout according to their beliefs concerning the stars.

At the eastern entrance to the lodge a post is placed, representing the Morning Star God of the day and of fire and light. Another post is placed at the west, which represents the Goddess of the night, the Evening Star. Each day the light from the God enters the lodge and symbolically 'fertilises' the Goddess as it reaches the west point. Their original mating was said to have created the first human. In the north the North Star is represented and in the south, the Milky Way.

These lodges created a sacred space where rituals could be re-enacted concerning their beliefs as to their origins, stories would be told and prayers would be made to the gods of the cosmos and the earth for blessings on their lives, their crops and their animals.

Of course, more and more complex symbols and structures developed, until the early circular stone monuments, such as Stonehenge, slowly gave way to the building of highly complex domed temple structures, like the Blue Mosque in Istanbul. The dome eventually became the sacred structure common to all the ancient religions.

But however complex and esoteric the basis of temple design became, these structures were primarily designed to reflect the sacred principles of balance and cyclic movement in the universe. The purpose of building them according to the designs of the universe was to bring about the sought-after spiritual vision of one's own true self.

Looking at the ways in which the ancients designed their temples gives the modern-day designer of sacred gardens clues as to the way that they can create sacred spaces.

Above A beautiful coming-together of the square and the circle, the human and the spirit, and the inspiration for the knot garden on the right.

Top and below right The Museum of Garden History in London, England, has a fine example of parterre of *Buxus sempervirens*. This replica of an ancient knot garden was designed by the Marchioness of Salisbury and filled with historic plants. The shape follows the classical circle and square pattern, seen so often in ancient temple design. At the centre of this mandala is a contrasting topiary spiral, a universal symbol of growth in nature.

Sacred geometry

Many early cultures, such as the ancient Egyptians and the Celtic beliefs, represented in their sacred places the polar axis and the movement of the equinoxes, which create the seasons on earth. The seven planets circling the earth were said to have their own spheres, each sphere relating to a particular deity and having a musical tone of its own – hence the phrase, The Music Of The Spheres – and even particular angels associated with them.

The movements of the planets were revered and felt to be holy, holding the gods and goddesses who were thought to live in the heavens. Indeed, every religion acknowledged the sacredness of the heavens, which were thought to be the place of our shared origin.

I created the design for Broxmore Gardens in Hampshire, England, completely intuitively, without any particular knowledge at the time of sacred geometry and sacred numbers. After Robert Seaton gave me a brief for the garden (see page 22), I spent some time wandering around the rambling grounds on the winter misty afternoon of the winter solstice. I told him I would go home and 'dream' about the garden before commencing the plans.

The word 'dream' is not really adequate to describe the breadth of this process. Many spiritual teachers use this word to describe our otherwordly connection to our 'super-natural' intelligence and wisdom, our birthright, but one which is not often consciously available to us due to the predominantly 'left brain' conditioning which we receive in these modern times.

Aborigines call dreaming the 'essence' of an animal, plant or rock, the 'dreamtime' being the time when everything was created. North American Indians call the dream of an animal or person their 'soul story', a soul vision of the universe and reason for living.

When working on the designs for Broxmore, I felt drawn to experiment with circles within squares, particularly as the design was to be set within an almost square walled garden. I even purchased an especially large set of compasses in order to 'play' with the shapes at the large scale that I like to draw in.

I had sketched my ideas quickly, freehand, early one morning as an inspiration came to me. From these sketches I transferred my ideas on to a technically balanced landscape drawing, and overlaid a planting plan.

I felt it important, energetically, to ensure that the garden was designed around the central ancient well and wanted to keep the well open to the air, even though it was no longer being used for drawing water from.

I drew radiating paths leading out from the central meditation arbor, while a north, south, east, west cross-axis bisected the centre. Circular paths sat within an inner square and more organically shaped paths meander outside the main circle: one of these outer paths is distinctly feminine in shape.

As time passed and the garden began to take shape, I had a chance to reflect on the hidden meanings held in the design that I had created intuitively and from a point of beauty. It has fascinated me to see the similarity of form to that of traditional monastic gardens – even the 'flowery mead' of these gardens finding its equivalent in the wild flower meadow along the east walls of Broxmore. At the time this design was made I had

Right The outline of the garden plan laid out at Broxmore Gardens. The meditation centre and concentric circles can be seen and the main North/South axis walkway, lined with clipped *Quercus Ilex* trees.

Far right The statue of Pan playing his pipes at the end of the long walkway to the 'fire' area.

simply used shapes that pleased me and had been unaware of the relationships that they had with monastic gardens; that these gardens were very often designed around a central water feature, for instance.

The garden at Broxmore is beautiful and the design has intrigued all of those involved in its making, but particularly Art Howe, a researcher in sacred geometry and the histories of Glastonbury. Art believes that 'Anyone who finds pleasure in whiling away the time with a compass and a ruler will eventually understand that geometry is the grandfather of all arts and sciences.'

Art Howe made certain interesting observations and calculations with regard to the numbers held within the drawings of the garden. He said that when he first saw the garden design he was struck by its feminine shapes, which he said lead to a womb shape giving birth to the central well area. After calculating its scale he discovered it to be a perfect size for a stylized recreation of the original wattle and daub circular chapel at Glastonbury, reputed to have been built by Joseph of Arimathea and to have been lost in the reformation of 1539.

The original rose pattern at the centre of my design had eight directional arrows. These arrows perfectly contained the octagonal geometry of the Glastonbury floor. At Robert Seaton's request a central arbor was constructed as a scaled-down version of the chapel, using the same sacred numbers and geometry.

The observations of a scholar of sacred number and geometry, such as Art Howe, are fascinating when applied to an intuitively created design. Whether one takes significance of all these points is up to the observer. The garden has a beauty in its own right and needs no such under-standing. It has, however, an energy which seems bigger than the sum of its parts and as such is a mysterious place, seeming to hold an energy traditional to a temple garden.

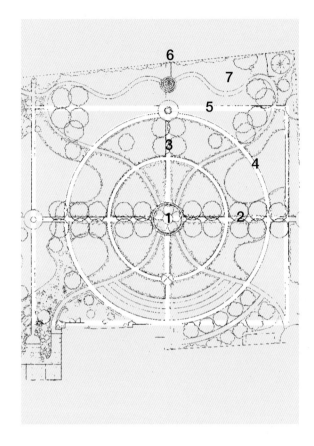

Above The ancient shape of the circle and the square can be seen clearly in the modern design for Broxmore Gardens. Combining the square and circle represents the meeting of spirit and matter, mankind and God, the sacred meeting of opposites.

1 The circular centre where the old well was retained and an arbour covers a meditation space.
2 The central north-south axis of the garden is lined with *Quercus ilex* trees
3 The central east-west axis, moving from the ornamental vegetable area in the east to a large feature urn in the west, and flanked with brightly coloured beds of dahlias.

4 The large circle within the outer square, creating a long walkway which passes through colour-themed areas of roses and shrubs.
5 The inner perimeter square, the brick paths of which take the visitor on a walk from the jacuzzi, to the ornamental pond, the fire pit, the flowery mead, the sunny sitting area, the spacious greenhouse and past the vegetable beds, before returning to the house.
6 The exit out of the garden through a secret gateway in the arched water grotto into the surrounding woods.
7 The flowery mead with the meandering mown path running through it.

Left The hand-made tiles on the floor of Broxmore Garden's circular meditation arbor. The cast-metal grid over the well is decorated with plant symbols of the four seasons.

The astrological symbols for Cancer, Leo and Virgo can be seen next to two of the seats, which have silver-leaved plants sacred to the Virgin Mary trailing from the raised bed behind them. Beyond, the orange and red dahlia beds can be glimpsed along with the path leading to the grotto in the garden walls, which in turn leads to the surrounding woodland.

Squares and circles

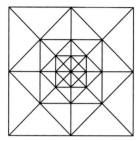

The square is absent in all almost of nature's creations and is primarily dreamed up in the human mind and represented in Man's creations. The circle, however, has always been considered as godlike, in that it can be all encompassing. Seen three-dimensionally it is a sphere, the same shape as the planets and the Earth.

Most representations of the world of the spirit are circular, offering a visual metaphor for wholeness and eternity. So, combining the square and circle is symbolic of the meeting of spirit and matter, mankind and God, mankind and the earth; the sacred meeting of opposites.

This combination of the square and circle is the foundation of the sacred architecture of ancient temples found all over Eastern Europe, Greece, Italy and Central Asia. Today this common foundation seems to present a remarkable unity of thought, philosophy and spirituality between religions, whereas we, in the modern age, seem to be endlessly at odds with one another's beliefs.

Leonardo da Vinci's famous drawing, *The proportions of the human figure after Vitruvias*, shows the figure of a man within a circle held within a square. The perimeter of this square is almost, but mysteriously never exactly, equal to the circumference of the circle.

'Squaring the circle' – making a square with a perimeter equal to the circumference of a circle contained within it – is a theoretical impossibility, but attempting to do so is, due to the sacred nature of the relationship between the circle and the square, a meditation on God.

An example of a modern-day garden that uses squares and circles in its design is one that was created at Fairfield in Surrey by the photographer John Glover. Sacred geometry defines all aspects of the design of this beautiful garden, which has been oriented to the polar axis – the traditional way to begin to define a sacred space.

The geometry itself is a simple square that gradually reduces in upon itself by making the points of each new square start in the middle of the sides of the previous larger square, as shown in the diagram on the left. The sacred number used is four, the number traditionally associated with the square and direction, and with the Earth itself. The central part of the garden design, the most sacred space, is a circular pond.

By finding a simple way to establish a circle within the geometry of the square, John aimed to create a sacred garden that drew on the ancient wisdom of sacred numbers and, symbolically, the 'squaring of the circle'. The circle within the square represents the creation of heaven on earth, the Garden of Eden, the sacred place itself.

The garden also has an Indian mandala-like quality with 'doors' and paths leading from all the cardinal compass points: the West door was chosen as the spot to position a seat to sit and contemplate the garden. In India, mandalas are used as a visual device to assist meditation. They encourage the initiate to gradually quieten the mind and progress towards the central stillness of the design. Indian temples are based on exactly the same principles, so a garden seemed like a very natural interpretation of this idea.

The garden also seems to have a Christian feel to it, with the shape of the cross being clearly shown, but this shape can also be seen as a more universal symbol.

The pond in the centre of the garden is designed to be the focus for contemplation of the garden, especially when the sun sparkles on the water and the flowers of the red water-lily open.

The pond and the plants have been chosen to attract wildlife, such as dragonflies and newts, and, in fact, the water contains a whole range of pond life. Birds come here to drink and bathe and, on a warm summer day, the garden is alive with the hypnotic buzz of pollinating insects and the scents of herbs.

Right This small-scale mandala-like garden combines both Christian and Hindu symbolism. Strong lines in the design draw the eye to the magic of the jewel-like pond in the centre, where the sacred shape of the circle sits.

The golden proportion – the search for harmony and balance

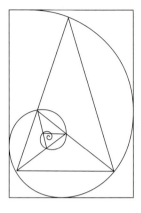

When I was at school I found most mathematics trying and uninspiring, until I began to study geometry. I found, to my surprise, that I was suddenly very good at this kind of maths. It was only later, when I became a garden designer, that I started to understand how the visual nature of geometry appealed to my very visual way of perceiving the world.

Only later still did I realize that the ancient mathematicians had a deeply spiritual perspective on their discoveries and that their work was descriptive of the creative way the universe works to manifest planets, landscapes, plants, creatures and particularly human beings.

By bringing to life some of the stuffy maths we learnt at school, by making it simple, I want to show how sacred places have been built using these principles. I also want to show how we can use the same principles in the design of our gardens and sacred outdoor spaces in the twenty-first century.

In ancient Greece, when for some there was probably all the time in the world to play around with rulers and compasses, the discovery of the golden proportion was made. The golden proportion is a ratio that describes a measure of difference. A dictionary definition describes the golden proportion as 'the way of wisdom and safety, the place between two extremes'.

The golden proportion is a numerical way of showing how experiencing a point between two extremes can bring about unity and wisdom. It demonstrates numerically the relationship to unity (The Divine) through the asymmetrical dynamic power of phi. This relationship is why the Greeks called it the golden or 'divine' proportion and why Johannes Kepler, the formulator of the laws of planetary motion, referred to it as one of the 'jewels of geometry'. The box on page 83 explains a little about ratios and proportions, how the golden proportion is created and how it is used to create other pleasing shapes.

The golden proportion in design
The Golden Mean Spiral is the beautiful spiral that can be drawn using the logarithmic progression of numbers, discovered by the 13th-century mathematician Fibonacci – it is sometimes called the Fibonacci series. These numbers can be used to draw beautifully proportioned spirals ideal for design purposes.

Above A spiral being created through the drawing of successive golden triangles that were themselves created within a golden rectangle.

Right The central seed head of a yellow dahlia, developing in a perfect golden spiral form.

Addition makes a thing bigger, but multiplication, although simply another form of addition, can bring about acceleration – a leap of growth, such as that of the rapidly accumulating cells when seeds germinate, or the sudden understanding of an idea or concept, or, in a spiritual context, a moment of enlightenment.

The Golden Mean Spiral, created from the numbers generated by phi, shows this geometric growth leap in a visual form. The spiral growth pattern can be seen throughout the universe. The Golden Mean Spiral, where the geometric increase is that of phi, can be seen in nature in the shape of a nautilus shell. Often shown in the hand of the dancing Hindu God, Shiva, this shell is one of the instruments through which he is said to have created the world.

This logarithmic spiral of growth can be traced in the growth of the human foetus and is also present in the growth patterns of plants. The patterns of the seeds in a sunflower are also determined by this principle, having 34 or 89 anti-clockwise spirals of seeds and an overlay of 55 clockwise spirals.

Above An example of Gertrude Jekyll's planting of flowing colours within a long herbaceous border.

Ratios, proportions, phi and the golden proportion
A ratio is a measure of difference, a comparison of two things. It is an expression of the way one thing is different to another and is therefore representative of the way we perceive and discriminate. A proportion is more complicated, as it concerns relationships of likenesses between two ratios; for example one item is to the second item as the third item is to the fourth.

Phi, the 21st letter of the Greek alphabet is used to describe the unique three-number proportion constructed from two numbers, known as the golden or 'divine' proportion. This golden proportion is obtained by dividing a line (a–b) into two at a point (c) whereby the whole line (a–b) is longer than the first part (a–c) in the same proportion as (a–c) is longer than the second part (c–b).

A series of golden rectangles can be created using the golden proportion and can eventually be used to create a perfect logarithmic spiral. A series of golden triangles can also be used to create a logarithmic spiral, like the one shown on page 82.

The golden mean has fascinated mathematicians and artists for centuries, it was considered by Plato to be the key to the cosmos and is seen repeatedly in growth patterns in nature.

Phi is known as the 'golden' proportion because it creates three from two and it can be seen to parallel the Mystery of The Holy Trinity, that is the Three that is Two.

Finding the golden proportion in ourselves

To the Greeks there was no separation between the sciences, and mathematics was allowed to flow seamlessly into philosophy, thereby allowing the perception of universal truths through the study of numbers. This propogated their belief in the sacredness of numbers. To the Greeks the sacred golden proportion was a numerical expression of the rhythm of the universe, creating itself and everything within it.

The golden proportion can be found abundantly in nature and in sacred art from India, Egypt, China and Islam. It is in the gothic art of the Middle Ages and prevalent in the works of the Renaissance. It was discovered independently in many different cultures and was seen as having sacred significance in them all.

In this modern age, we seem to have lost sight of many of the universal sacred laws. One way we can feel less separated from them is through experiencing ancient sacred architecture, where the laws of harmony and proportion were invariably used in their design.

Chartres Cathedral is a fine example of this kind of sacred architecture. Its curved interior design is based on the calculations of the golden proportion and the visitor may note that, unlike inside modern buildings, the feelings experienced here bring a sense of an infinite existence.

Simply by looking at the line and triangle drawing of the golden proportion, we may sense the reason why this measure contains universal teachings of balance and harmony, useful in many fields from conflict resolution to garden design.

There has always been a quest for balance in both art and spirituality and this quest can be seen in so many creative works. Gertrude Jekyll's herbaceous borders were designed and planted to flow from one bright extreme of colour, through into gentler colours in between and back into brightness again.

But to understand the inner significance of the golden mean fully, we need to consider the extremes between our inner and outer world. In a perfect state of meditation, the object, ourself and the divine we are contemplating become one and the same, the middle place, no longer separated from the extremes of each other – an experience of Unity.

In the past, knowledge of this godlike golden proportion was known to have great spiritual significance and the artistic expression of it was both suppressed and its application kept secret by the church.

Today this knowledge helps to fuel many people's understanding of a spiritual, evolving universe, indeed it leads them towards an understanding of a belief in a guided process of evolution and an infinite relatedness to the perfection of the source of creation, the Divine.

Below The design of the meandering, flowing paths in The Feng Shui Garden at Hampton Court Palace Flower show were inspired by the ever-turning, twisting and curving lines and patterns in our universe. The curving form of the diving woman sculpture, *Free Spirit* by Janis Ridley, also mirrors the curves found within the nautilus shell, shown right.

Right The spiralling development of the structure of the nautilus shell demonstrates the Fibonacci series of logarithmic progression and creates a wonderful form.

The New Geometry

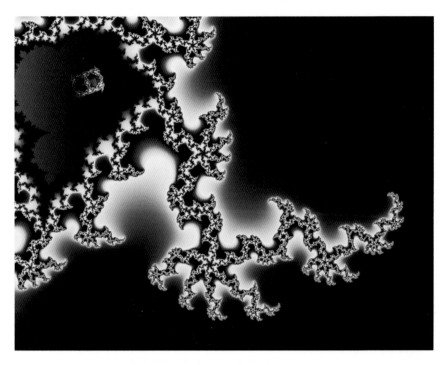

Above An endlessly self-repeating image within a computer-generated fractal. Fractals can be created on screen through the use of numerical equations, thereby allowing scientists to become artists and create stunning images, strangely resonant with those found within nature.

Right Looking up into the sky through the tracery of leaves in a tree canopy. This is a natural self-repeating fractaline formation, familiar to all of us and a source of inspiration to anyone who has ever laid under a group of trees.

The modern scientific world has been trying to understand the way nature and the universe work, so that they can develop laws and predictive methods and eventually learn how to control nature. This began to be seen as a task without end. However, since the 1960s there have been some exciting new additions to geometry describing nature.

This new geometry shows nature to have less precision than that suggested by the golden proportion and the traditional geometry of the classroom. It is far more chaotic and unpredictable than scientists had ever dreamt.

We only have to study a tree or wave movements in the sea to realize that these are complex, dynamic systems whose development depends on infinite factors, which in turn are influenced by yet more. Edward Lorenz, an American meteorologist, discovered that it is impossible to predict the weather accurately. Weather systems are affected by billions of ever-changing factors – even tiny ones, such as the heat coming from a car somewhere in India, can

lead to a completely unpredictable occurrence, throwing a prediction out. He concluded that we live in a chaotic universe that is unimaginably rich, highly sensitive and completely unpredictable.

Natural systems are often subject to 'positive feedback' whereby the smallest occurrence can lead to a catastrophic reaction, such as the movement of a pebble giving rise to a landslide. These systems are affected by everything within them and as such are 'holistic'; even the Dalai Lama says that somewhere in America will be affected by the flight of a single mosquito in China.

In the 1960s and 1970s a new geometry was invented by an IBM researcher called Benoit Mandelbrot. He called it 'fractal' geometry, coming from the words 'fractured' and 'fractional', meaning broken into units. Fractal describes the uneven, broken or crinkly structures that arise in nature as a result of dynamic and chaotic activity.

Mandelbrot developed numerical equations that he ran through a computer continuously by 'feeding' their own result back to them, thereby creating a positive feedback system. It is only in the modern age of computers that the massive calculations needed to turn positive feedback into self-repeating images has become possible.

These equations have been able to generate beautiful computer images that show worlds within worlds. This 'self-similarity' can be seen in everything from the pattern of fallen leaves on the ground, to the tracery of blood vessels around our lungs. Mandelbrot images can also be used to model real natural systems, such as the projected formation of sands around coastlines and the turbulent flowing of air in weather systems.

The divide between order and chaos has always been viewed as present in the Divine force. Mandelbrot's discoveries enable us to view the order in our chaotic universe, and help us to accept that the universe is truly uncertain. As designers it is this beauty that is intriguing and we can use it to great effect in our work.

Above left to right Self-repeating forms in the garden, from the dew on *Plectranthus argentatus* to an *Allium cristophii* flower head; the star-like petal patterns of a pink dahlia and *Allium nigrum*; ornamental cabbage and liriodendron leaves revealing the pattern of the veins.

Landforms

Above and right Views of the landscape created in the 18th century by Charles Bridgeman. Today it is referred to as a 'landform' and is indeed a very contemporary landscape, though unlike today's landforms, this one was dug by hand.

A remarkable and strangely contemporary-looking large-scale 'landform' is that designed by the 18th-century landscape designer, Charles Bridgeman, at Claremont in Surrey, England. Bridgeman also designed landforms in Buckinghamshire and Oxfordshire, but the vast, turfed amphitheatre at Claremont is one of the few to survive. His dramatic work is being rediscovered and is influencing modern designers.

The architectural historian, Charles Jenks, plays an important role in the wave of thinking sweeping through today's scientific and artistic worlds. He is excited by what he describes as the 'jumps' made in our evolutionary story, the fractaline forms in nature described by Mandelbrot and the many artistic interpretations of this new story that may possible.

In his book *The Architecture of the Jumping Universe* Jenks describes how contemporary cosmologists see the universe as not ordered, but complex, chaotic and yet 'self organising', and from which we have evolved.

These patterns of cosmic development are becoming equated with the 'patterns of God'. When we observe these in the form of fractals or other designs we may experience a sense of awe, while feeling their strange familiarity.

Charles says that this 'outer' language of the universe needs an equivalent 'inner' language in art and design. His role has been to create, with his late wife Maggie Keswick, a ground-breaking landscaped garden in Dumfriesshire, Scotland, called the Garden of Cosmic Speculation.

The garden has some interesting resonances with Bridgeman's Claremont landscape, certainly in terms of scale and its wave-like forms, now known to be the basic shapes of the universe.

In Jenks's garden the new cosmic codes are expressed in a poetic and individual way, drawing on the 'Op-Art' forms seen in the 1960s and creating a 'landscape of waves', amplifying the flowing way in which nature organizes itself.

A series of ponds were dug with bulldozers, which left in their wake shapes that caught Maggie and Charles's attention. Charles says that nature is basically curved, warped, undulating, beautifully crinkly and often folded in on itself, like the shapes left by the machines.

They were able to include these ideas of twists, folds and waves of energy and created a great spiral mound, which leads the visitor around the landscape in a most unusual way: you need to walk back and forth in order to climb the mound, just as you travel life's journey.

From these cosmogenic concepts, Jenks seems to define an emerging spiritual culture and proposes a new direction for the contemporary arts. His gardens are designed to tell the story of the expanding universe, our generation being the first to be able to understand this chronologically.

He believes the universe to be the most significant entity from which to draw style, as it is the form from which we originate and its story can unify our many cultural and spiritual beliefs.

Designing with universal patterns

The discovery of the golden proportion and the new geometry of fractals shows that there is both a curiosity about the formation of the universe and an instinctive aesthetic sense that responds to this information and is driven to recreate it in art.

Nature rarely creates straight lines or even a perfect curve. Traditional and modern geometry, although helpful in getting us to draw, will, I feel, ultimately make way for the instinctive dancing curve of the natural hand movement. Fractaline images will keep inspiring us to repeat our finest lines, creating shapes within shapes – a characteristic of some of the finest artists.

I rarely have the desire to design with sharp and accurate geometric precision, but prefer to begin freehand, by instinct, inspired by the organic shapes that appear as my hand flows. Precision can always be introduced later as a means to assure the design works technically, but I have to commence by allowing my organic process to flow through my body and hand on to the paper. Music's harmonies and flowing rhythms are of invaluable assistance in this process.

The soulful garden will, of course, take inspiration from the universe. The celebrated contemporary designer, Kathryn Gustafson, has made the patterns of Orion and the moon into her leading forms in the Arthur Ross terrace at the New York Planetarium. Water jets and fibre optic lights are arranged in the pattern of the Orion star cluster and moon shadows cast by the domed building are reflected in the design of the granite and lawn surfaces of the terrace.

As Charles Jenks says, the Universe is the single, creative, unfolding event providing narrative and grounding. It is only the story of the universe which can satisfy our emerging global culture.

Left The sweeping twists of raked gravel are emphasized by sunlight in this Japanese Zen garden. They are a minimal representation of the energy moving within the landscape, and similar to the wave patterns thought to make up the universe in which we live and from which we were created.

Plant spirit ·

Plants in the sacred garden are the essential mediators with the world of spirit. Apart from providing all the glory and aesthetic pleasure expected in a beautiful garden, they also bring something far deeper.

What is plant spirit

Top left Arisaema japonicum catching just a touch of light in its shady, woodland setting.

Top right Alchemilla mollis covered in raindrops.

Far right The unfurling fronds of the fern *Matteuccia struthiopteris*. Three uniquely different forms of plants choosing to live in the same environment and yet each beautiful detail and individual chemical constituent being determined by its own cellular DNA code.

When we plant flowers, shrubs and trees in our gardens, we often choose them for their colouring or for their ability to thrive in our soil or climate. However, we should also look beyond these qualities and examine the spiritual nature of plants.

The body of every plant, like our own bodies, carries its own unique genetic code, in the form of the DNA held in every cell. The magical code for life carried by this spiralling form determines the inheritance of every aspect of a plant, from its environmental requirements to its flower colour, the texture of its leaves and the taste of its fruit.

Rupert Sheldrake, the biochemist and prolific writer, has proposed that other characteristics are also inherited, recognizing that the true nature of plants – and, indeed, of all organisms – cannot be fully understood by examining scientific data alone. His theory of morphic resonance proposes that

nature itself has memory in the form of an 'invisible blueprint' and this is as profoundly influential as the cellular, material DNA. He says that these 'morpho-genetic fields' could be responsible for the inheritance of certain characteristics that are not identifiable genetically and that do not arise from behavioural influence.

Certainly, plants today are recognized for their chemical constituents and their resultant ability to heal, but there are also a broad range of essences and aromatherapy oils that are used for subtle results, and there is no way to determine the biochemical ingredients responsible.

Possibly, each plant has its own specific type of energy field and contacting the sacred nature of this field gives access to special qualities and secret worlds, whether through use as medicines or through simply being in contact with them.

Healing with the spirit of plants

Left A traditional herb garden at Cranbourne Manor in Dorset, England, where culinary and medicinal herbs grow within low hedges of santolina and lavender, and rub shoulders with roses, enclosed by a large, clipped yew hedge for protection.

Right and far right below Ancient olive trees growing in Greece. Olive flowers are used to create a Bach Flower Remedy for the subtle relief of exhaustion.

Far right, top to bottom Fields of lavender, the source of the universally useful healing oil of lavender. *Echinacea purpurea*, the root of which has been discovered to dramatically increase our immune systems, preventing our susceptibility to colds and influenza.

Much is spoken about the healing power of plants. Their aromas come from their oil essences, which are steam-distilled from different parts of the plant to create substances with their own unique chemical constituents and subtle energy signature. When used either in massage oils, baths or simply as body or room scents, these essential essences can switch on a part of the brain, body or spirit and bring about physical, emotional and spiritual effects.

Another way to use the mysterious qualities of a plant is through flower essences. These differ from essential oils in the way they are produced. The flowers are usually soaked in spring water, in natural sunlight, so that the vibration of the flower becomes present in the water and is available for use.

English physician and author, Dr Edward Bach in the 1930s stated in his book *The Seven Helpers* that, in the presence of nature, disease has no power, and he repeatedly said that the way of nature is to be found in the fields. Although his flower remedies have been investigated often,

to describe their effects is difficult to put into words, and they need to be sensed personally.

Another healing system that uses plants is homeopathy. This practice uses various substances from the plant, animal and mineral worlds, which are diluted to such a degree that the original substance cannot be chemically traced. Indeed, this healing art uses the energy signature, or what I call the 'spirit' of a substance, as its healing source.

We may decide that it is the fragrance of a specific flower that enables a particular meditation or mood to descend upon us. The science of aromatherapy has shown that fragrances can affect us on a deep, emotional level, with some plant aromas having the ability to evoke a state of spiritual reflection, or even quite specific states of awareness.

The careful placing and combination of fragrant flowers is an important consideration in a sacred garden. Too many different scents within one area of the garden, for instance, may confuse the senses of the visitor.

In pursuit of plant spirit

In the pursuit of the spirit of plants, I have found that it is only when we spend time in stillness and close proximity to them that we experience their mysterious gifts. Sometimes, their secrets are only revealed in their particular home environment. This is the way Bach discovered his essences – by walking in nature.

To create a garden that includes the spirit world, we need to explore far more than the aesthetic art of placing plants. We need to move beyond our constant desire to maximize their physical performance in the garden. Plants can change our state of mind, alter our consciousness or evoke an energy or deity from the world of spirit, mediating a transcendent experience.

The invisible world of plants can be accessed in many different ways and it is this very mysterious aspect of trees, herbs, flowers, seeds and fruits that is the realm of the shamans, spirit healers and artists.

Plants and deities

When I spend time in the garden of Angie Avis, in Devon, England, in midsummer, as the light begins to fade, I can see why she has chosen the many hues of pink, white and magenta in her deep, double herbaceous borders. She blends roses, lavender, diascia, artemesia and foxgloves in much the same way as the celebrated garden designer Gertrude Jekyll might have done, but instead, particularly celebrates the glory of pink.

Angie's garden has an area intended for the celebration of the spirit of Venus, and when the evening arrives, the brighter tones of magenta-pink come alive. In the double herbaceous border, the *Lychnis coronaria* and *Geranium* 'Anne Folkard' sparkle like fairy lights, while a glimpse of the statue of Venus can be seen at the end of the central grass path.

In the daytime, however, when the sun warms the petals of the many pink and white old-fashioned roses, a heady scent provides

a different experience of plant spirit. The smell of roses has always been associated with the spirit of Venus, the Roman goddess of love and her qualities of both sensuous and spiritual love. The Romans and the Egyptians understood the sensuous and magical qualities of the rose. The Egyptian queen, Cleopatra, is said to have prepared a room knee-deep in rose petals in order to seduce Mark Anthony.

A garden of roses evokes this spirit of Venus and creates within us a strange feeling of heady lightness. If we surrender to its scent, it will send our spirits drifting away with the feelings of a million love songs.

By complete contrast to the heady realms of the Venusian rose garden, the spirit of plants can also be sought in the wilder places. A very different spirit may be found in a shady piece of land, where mosses grow, ferns catch every little glimpse of light and not a single coloured flower is apparent. A garden created in such a place may be where the company of the green spirit of Pan might be courted.

Whilst Pan's omnipresent spirit can be felt even in the cities, his wild and earthy presence can be experienced easily in the leafy undergrowth of shady spaces under trees. To woo this sacred presence, try a rich and heavy planting, dense and chaotic, more wild in style than the cultivated border. This is the spirit of the Greenwood, of the ancient forests, rich and mysterious, playful and unpredictable, the very essence of the raw spirit of nature.

Meetings such as these are discussed in *The Findhorn Garden*, a collection of writings edited by Sir George Trevellyan, which concerns the spiritual perspectives of the community of Findhorn in Scotland. Pan is described as one of the elementals, those mysterious energies associated with the plant world, which are able to be experienced only when one is in a state of heightened awareness.

Right The climbing rose 'Blush Rambler', a densely clustering rose of the softest pink. The rose was sacred to the Egyptians and the Romans and was known to be a potion in magical arts of love.

The relationship of plants to light, and of ourselves to plants, is undisputed – they are our prime source of nourishment and breathable air. The co-evolution of ourselves and plants on this planet could be very significant in terms of our relationship and response to light and colour.

This chapter will talk about seeing and feeling with senses other than our eyes. However, sight is the most immediate of all our physical senses and colour is a primary factor affecting mood. By shifting our moods and feelings, we can begin to 'see' more clearly with our other senses.

All designers know that light and colour have a profound affect on our well-being, but careful use of colour can also influence our sensitivity to

the world of spirit. The idea of colour therapy isn't new and is, in fact, an ancient healing technique, probably first practiced by the ancient Egyptians, who used gems to direct coloured sunlight on to those who were ill.

Today, colour is used by some alternative health practitioners to balance the body's energy. Different hues relate to various emotional and physical states, and although some of the theory behind colour therapy remains scientifically unproven, there are ancient teachings, such as the Hindu/tantric chakra system, that describe the energy fields around the human body.

The chakra system describes a wave of different colours present around particular areas

Left to right
Leucanthemum x *superbum*
'Aglaia', touched by mauve
thalictrum flowers. White
is the colour of the crown
chakra. This is the energy
centre which has the
capacity to open to the
so-called higher spiritual
realms beyond that of
the earth – the body's
connection with Spirit itself.

The chakra known as the
third eye is said to resonate
with the colour purple.
One of the flowers chosen
for this part of the garden
were the violas, such as this
purple winter pansy (*Viola*).

The throat chakra is usually
visualized as a vivid blue.
Blue is not the most
common of colours and
bright blues are rare, but
Gentiana acaulis has petals
of a blue which is true to
this energy centre.

The heart chakra is sensed
around the middle of the
chest. Two colours are
thought to resonate with
this zone, soft green and
gentle pink. A whole range
of flowers could, of course,
be used in this part of the
garden. Here *Tulipa* 'Peach
Blossom' perfectly
combines the two.

The chakra of the solar
plexus is said to be the
centre of the will and is
found just under the
ribcage. The colour of this
chakra is bright orange.
Below the solar plexus
chakra is the 'womb'
chakra, which is said to be
the centre of our personal
creativity and is a rich
orange in colour.
These Icelandic poppies
(*Papaver nudicaule*) contain
both orange and yellow
flowers and could be used
in the area of the chakra
garden where these two
centres meet.

We always have to return to
the source of our human
energy and at the base of
the spine is said to reside
our sleeping 'kundalini'.
Here the beautiful red field
poppy (*Papaver rhoeas*)
with its rich, red petals and
black stamens is a perfect
representation of this zone.

of the body. Some people describe this as our 'dream body', visible only to a few sensitive people who are able to see these colours. Different colours are associated with different chakras and areas of the body.

This ancient knowledge is an exciting consideration when designing a garden with plants. At Chalice Well Gardens, in Glastonbury, Gloucestershire, it was decided to create just such a garden and my help was asked in designing the scheme.

There had always been a beautiful stretch of herbaceous planting flanking the path to the well itself, but this was in need of renewal. The idea of transforming this into a place where visitors could relate the colours of their own energy field with those displayed in the garden through flower and leaf colour seemed very exciting.

In truth, this was to be a sacred version of the traditional English herbaceous border. Plants such as roses, irises and lilies are particularly sacred in Chalice Well Gardens, sacred to the Virgin Mary in the Christian tradition and to the Goddess in the pagan tradition. Such plants have been given an important place in the new planting scheme, but the real challenge was to weave a tapestry of leaf and flower colours from deep reds through orange, yellows, pinks/greens, blue, purple/magenta to white – the different colours of the chakras.

Although the main outline on the planting plan formed the skeleton structure, careful interweaving of subtle bridging plants needed to be artfully placed to blend, for instance, the difficult contrast between the yellow and pink area. Here, pink ballerina roses and yellow Lady's mantle were bridged with the apricot hues of *Verbascum* 'Helen Johnson'. Likewise, the silver leaves of *Eryngium giganteum* and *Buddleia alternifolia* were combined with the white flowers of climbing 'Iceberg' roses, allowing a bridge between the blue and the white areas.

Chalice Well Gardens is a fine example of the potency of flowers. By carefully considering the colours of the plants we would love to have in our gardens, we can create particular atmospheres and intensify the sense of spirit.

Our choice of plants, and hence the availability of colour in the garden, is continually expanding. Every year, the flower shows boast of the arrival of newly created hybrids or of new flowers imported from foreign lands.

Choosing colours can feel confusing, so let's begin with a look at the way I have used the colour of the plant world to create a sense of balance and beauty by combining it with aspects of the ancient spiritual system of feng shui.

If sacred space can be created at a flower show, where thousands of people hustle and bustle through everyday, then it can be created anywhere. This is exactly what was achieved in The Feng Shui Garden at the Hampton Court Palace Flower Show. Working primarily with the colour of plants, I found that by following the system of the *ba gua* as a design tool, harmonious use of colour was simplified.

A wave of floral and foliar colour ribboned around the garden, starting with bright reds in the South area that met and flowed into orange/bronze and yellow, then into silver/yellow and gold and blues, blacks and purples, until, in the North area, it flowed into greens, browns, bronze and back to rich red. These are the colours of the *ba gua*, each one associated with a compass point and an aspect of life. This system lends itself well to being used in a garden design scheme, but once again, requires the careful use of bridging plants to bring about harmonious plant groupings.

Plants seem to 'sing' when they are placed for beauty and sacredness in this way. Something magical happens when a system like the *ba gua* is used to help the designer, and the significance of the colour of plants is celebrated.

Right Covering the Chalice Well itself is a beautiful timber cover decorated with the ancient symbol of the Vesica Pisces, a symbol of the feminine principles of the womb and the moon.

The shaman's tale

Colour is an important part of the deep effect of plants on our spirit, and yet it is just one aspect of the subtle nature of plants that we can experience. We may dream of plants in colour, we may even recall a sweet smell of a certain fragrance when waking from a dream, but as ordinary gardeners seeking to experience the dreaming world of plant spirit, we might become deeply inspired by listening to the tales of the shaman.

No longer are shamans popularly referred to as witch doctors. Today, a return to a respect and fascination for their now rare skills and magic is being re-discovered all over the world. Theirs is a very ancient art, with every culture and country in the world having their own unique history of shamanic healing practices.

When Martín Prechtel, once a Guatamalan village chief and shaman, recalls his experiences with plants, he tells of how the shaman is 'sought out' or chosen by a plant. A vision of a plant may come to the chosen shaman in a dream, or during a ceremony, and Martín says they usually appear in the form of a woman whose clothing may be similar in appearance to the plant itself.

He tells of a time when illness hit the area where he lived. His skills as a healer were much in demand, but one man continued to be unresponsive to his work, no matter what he tried. The patient's health was in deep decline and Martín knew that he had to try something new.

He fell into an exhausted sleep and dreamed that he was walking along a familiar coastline when a woman, dressed in yellow, appeared from the bushes and shouted to him, 'Martín, I hate you!' He asked her why this was, and she accused him of never making love to her sister! As Martín pleaded that he knew nothing of her sister, he saw another, younger and smaller, woman appear, dressed in white. She walked towards him and they walked away together.

Martín awoke from the dream and quickly realized that on a coastline he knew, there were

two varieties of mimosa, one with yellow flowers and another smaller variety whose flowers were white. He asked a traveller to bring him supplies of this particular white-flowered mimosa from the coast, and the medicine from the plant rapidly healed his patient.

Martín says that a shaman may only 'partner' very few plants in his or her life, and maybe even just one plant in their life as a healer. He says it is important to realize that the plant chooses the person, not they the plant. The spirit relationship between the shaman and the plant is the healing factor.

He tells a story of a woman shaman who treated everyone with burdock, whatever their illness. Unlike the herbalist who chooses a particular plant for a specific purpose, this shaman worked with the energy or 'spirit' of burdock. The partnership of plant and shaman is the medicine, and this woman could therefore bring about the healing of a whole variety of ailments with just one plant.

Although the specialized healing skill of the shaman is unlikely to be one readily available to us, the experiences of plant spirit in dreams, daydreams and meditations can guide the gardener of the sacred garden when choosing plants. This can deepen the special relationship between gardener and plant and build meaning and excitement into the work of gardening.

Top right A frothy bright yellow mass of early spring flowering *Acacia longifolia* blossoms.

Far right The delicate white blossoms of *Acacia mellifera* var. *definens*.

Plant spirit in India – the Ayurvedic tradition

Above Euphorbias growing in a rocky, wild landscape. Plants growing wild are thought by the Ayurvedic tradition to be far more potent than those growing in towns and villages

Right Artemisia absinthium.

Far right, top to bottom Basil, bronze fennel, applemint and aloe vera. These are all used in Ayurvedic medicine, which is based on the belief that the same intelligences (or devas) from whom plants arose are responsible for the creation of humans. Particular plants resonate with certain parts of the human body and can return the 'memory' of a health, thereby bringing healing.

From the age of ten, Balaraj Maharishi trained with an Indian *saddhu* or holy man, instead of pursuing a formal education. This particular *saddhu* specialized in herbs and healing, the Ayurvedic tradition, and during his 15 years of training, Balaraj Maharishi experienced both enlightenment and the wisdom of working with the spirit of plants. After this training, as is the tradition in India, he travelled around the country from village to village, healing with herbs.

Balaraj would arrive at a 'wild' place outside the village, meditate there and contact the state of unity within himself, akin to the spirit of the wild plants found in the place. The plant spirits would reveal to him the ailments they could be used for. He would then go to the village and one by one 'see' which cures were needed by the villagers. Immediately he looked at each of them, he could 'see' their ailments, the local plant, or combination of plants, they needed and how they should be prepared.

The importance of plants growing in wild places is most significant in the Ayurvedic tradition, which says that plants grown in the wild are more powerful than cultivated ones. In this tradition, plants found wild in the area where you live are particularly important, for they contain what is needed for your cure.

Devatas, Sanskrit for the 'Laws of Nature', are the spiritual energies responsible for the physical creation of plants and also of the human body. A plant will contain an 'intelligence', which has the ability to wake up the memory of health in a particular part of the body.

The Ayurvedic tradition teaches that the *Devatas*, and hence the intelligence of the plants, is stronger in the wild places than in ones where large numbers of humans live, because humans tend to violate the Laws of Nature. Therefore, the plants found in the Himalayas will contain more of their essential 'intelligence' than those found, for instance, in Delhi.

In the Ayurvedic tradition, there are also rules that guide the picking of the plants. These are based on specific times in the moon's cycle, and even on the movements of the planets. Both of these are said to influence the strength of the plant's intelligence.

The stories of Balaraj Maharishi and that of the shaman, Martín Prechtel, describe two different ways in which a tradition that has been handed down to particular chosen and committed individuals brings the gifts of the world of plant spirit to ordinary people.

These stories inspire our work in the garden by bringing an awareness of plant spirits to us, even if we haven't been privileged or trained to actually 'see' or feel them ourselves. Remember that anyone can instinctively feel the presence of spirit using the four ordinary senses of smell, touch, taste and vision.

Plant spirit and the healer-gardener

I have met many people who, through experiences with their work or creativity, have been able to access the world of plant spirit in unique and personal ways. One of them is Helen Fletcher, an artist, photographer and psychotherapist, who tells of returning to a former home, transplanting plants in the garden and experiencing them intimately during painful periods in her life.

She explained, 'Moving my plants was such hard work, because I was ill at that time and also recovering from a broken relationship. I felt I was going to collapse after every push on the fork. I was burning up inside and felt crazy, in some kind of altered state.'

During the course of her work in the emerging garden, Helen's perception of it, and her relationship with it, changed dramatically. Looking back, she said, 'I now wanted a cottage-style garden, and so I planted more perennials, annuals and herbs, such as foxgloves, lobelias, Michaelmas daisies, love-in-a-mist, feverfews, different kinds of mint, marigolds, and wallflowers, among many others.

'Angelica, lovage, sage, lemon balm, marjoram, thyme and meadowsweet were placed in front of a wild honeysuckle that smelt heavenly in the evening summer breeze. When I had no room left, I started to grow plants in pots on the patio and bought armfuls of flowers for the garden table.

'I began to really learn the power of the herbs I was growing simply by being in their presence as living beings, rather than by drinking their teas. I remember the way that the first angelica shocked me, with its enormous bulbous pouch that seemed to explode open into flower heads. It made me think of angels taking flight.

'I loved watching the hairy comfrey flowers uncoiling. A hop, which grew and flowered on the right fence, looked vibrantly fertile, and its smell filled me with joy. I walked around touching, smelling, watching the bees collecting pollen and feeling such peace and pleasure.

'As a practicing iridologist, I was taking photos of eyes, so I started to take pictures of flowers as well. Because I used a macro lens, I could get right inside. I started to feel very connected spiritually with them. Often, I would experience bliss, a warm energy going through my heart, looking through my lens at a marvellous and wild landscape. It did not happen overnight, it was slow and unconscious. Year after year, spiritually the garden grew in me and I grew in the garden. I started to experience the obsession and addiction of gardening.

'Throughout two summers here, I wrote my dissertations on psychotherapy, read and took more photos of flowers. A friend who was studying feng shui informed me that where I sat day after day was traditionally known as the "learning space". I had moved the table to the left because I found I could relax and focus there. Behind me, on the wall, a large wind chime was singing and I remember feeling that it was calling angels. Just above here was my little meditation room, and the energy in here felt especially empowered by everything that was happening in the garden.

'By now I knew a lot about flower essences and used them often. I started to think that I was being attracted to the flowers I needed to be with. I felt compelled to grow busy lizzie and elecampane; their healing properties both related to my difficulty with breathing and the anxiety I was often suffering from.

'I slowly realized that it was my relationship with the garden and its spirits that had guided my choice of plants, as well as influenced my personal state. This relationship took years to establish and had been intensified and deepened by my personal experience of loss and growth.

'The pain I experienced during this period opened my heart and I felt that my soul started to speak as a result. Sometimes in the evening or early in the morning, I would catch the glowing energy of the garden emerging from the plants

and feel it travelling through my body. That, to me, was the spirit of the garden, a little piece of the magic of the land. I can still catch a glimpse of it in some of my photographs.'

Helen has recently moved away from this garden for good, to a new home, to be with her partner. When she was moving again, she discovered some dead nettles growing amongst the comfrey and somehow felt their support during this time of transition; even the most humble of garden weeds had become significant to her.

About the move, Helen says that she remembers thinking that by digging up her plants she could take her garden with her to her new home, believing that the spirits of the place would follow her there. She felt, however, that the magic actually stayed in her old garden where, in fact, it seemed to belong. This experience brought another lesson for Helen, to learn to let go and to welcome the adventure of starting to create a new garden with its own energy and its own relationship with the plant spirits.

Left *Digitalis purpurea* is an invaluable provider of digitalin, a medicine for the heart. The foxglove flower appears to beckon the eye inside it. The pathway, apparently designed to guide a bee's journey to the pollen, also draws the eye deeper inside its strangely patterned landscape. As Helen has experienced, the contemplation of flower patterns can bring their own profound and very personal experiences of healing.

The artist's story

Tracy Whitbread has exhibited her evocative and sumptuous flower paintings in British Columbia, Canada, and the United Kingdom. She says that she turned to flowers when visiting Canada, in order to find a scale that she could deal with. In fact, she found a landscape that contained everything within a single flower.

When she was young, she noticed how the flowers that her father grew brought her 'happy' feelings. She remembers, particularly, how he would place 'lady's slippers' on trays of gravel, and that she would see a lovely light and warmth exuding from them. These particular flowers brought her great comfort during a period in her childhood when her mother was in hospital.

Today, gardening, and the experience of being completely engrossed in the soil, begins the process of inspiration for Tracy's paintings. In springtime, weeding the garden reveals hidden life, an awesome experience of intimacy with the life of the plants. She feels completely excited by the tiny roots pushing out through the soil and the new shoots making their way to the surface, and feels once again like a child among the slipper flowers.

Before painting primroses in springtime, she will get down among them at ground level, to experience their scent and savour their very particular environment. She will take the plant into the studio and just look into it for a long time. She asks to become a 'channel' for the *deva* (spirit) of the plant. She asks, too, to be guided as how best to represent it and which colours to use. Sometimes she is surprised by the response.

Tracy can dream of painting *devas*, and of being among flowers and plants in the dream. Sometimes, extraordinary and indescribable atmospheres and happenings occur in a dream. When this happens, she recognizes the dream as being an experience of the plant *devas*.

Tracy will look at a flower from every angle, putting her face right into it, sensing its smell and feeling its colours. She feels that every flower has

a rhythm and a dance, and it was the observation of these unique and characteristic movements that led her to want to paint them.

The Red Hot Pokers, was painted at Burton Agnes Hall, in Yorkshire: these blooms were flowering in the garden when Tracy was artist in residence. This may have made a difference to her ability to experience *devas*, although she uses both cut and growing flowers in her work. She always asks the *devas* for 'permission' to paint, and sometimes will move on to another flower if she isn't getting a 'Yes' response.

Tracy calls her paintings 'Power Flowers'. She wants them to be exhibited in corporate situations, to bring the power of nature to people working in places surrounded by electricity, nylon carpets and computers, with the consequent stress that such an environment may bring. Having once worked as a graphic designer in a large company, Tracy speaks from experience.

'My paintings show the power of natural things, but especially flowers. I am interested in the power of their sensuality, rhythm and colour. Each flower has its own message and dance, which I aim to celebrate in my paintings.'

She paints on a large scale, to give people an experience of what is usually unseen – rather like being part of the insect world. Tracy hopes her work gives the flowers a voice. 'I believe that, now more than ever, we need to be paying attention to the earth and plants and flowers.'

Top right Tracy Whitbread's painting *The Red Hot Pokers* was created during one of her periods as artist in residency at Burton Agnes Hall in Yorkshire. This is a very special garden for Tracy, as she visited it when she was a child and even then knew she would spend time here one day. Her painting illustrates her own unique experience of the energy field pouring from these flowers.

Far right The inspiration for the work, red hot pokers, *Kniphofia rooperi*.

Trees

Trees are the big plant spirits of the land. Forests are the places in which humans sprang to life. Tree spirits are courted in indigenous communities to bring blessings to their people, and the shamans speak of the trees as being our brothers and protectors.

When creating a spirit garden, we can invite trees to act as the plant guardians they are in the wild landscape, the 'grandfathers' of the plant communities, who perceive the landscape from a completely different time perspective. According to the celebrated botanist Dr David Bellamy, studies of certain yew trees have shown some to have lived for over 3,000 years. I was once told that an oak tree takes 300 years to reach maturity, another 300 years to live its life as a mature tree and another 300 years to slowly die.

Great oak forests once grew right across western Europe. The oak tree was venerated as sacred, was seen as a great protector and believed to have been created by God. Through it sprang the whole human race. The Greek god, Zeus, and his wife, Hera, were known as the great god and goddess of the oak tree. One of the most sacred sites in Ancient Greece was Dodona, where Zeus was said to reside in an oak tree that had oracular powers. Indeed, the *devas*, or spirits, of trees are thought to be massive and godlike in scale.

Humans are physically, emotionally and spiritually tied to the nature of trees. Each culture and land has tales and myths associated with its own trees. Indeed, a pattern is said to be held within each tree that gives rise to the myths of the landscape they grow in.

In Devon, there are still to be found the remains of ancient, sacred groves that were known in the past as nematons, *nemus* being the Latin for sacred grove. In these areas, there still grows at least one of each type of tree sacred in the Celtic Pantheon of trees. Archaeologists have discovered that there once existed a huge area of forest in mid Devon, and there are still many place names to indicate that this was once a sacred forest. These include Broadnymet, Kings Nympton and Nymet Bridge.

When I visited the plantspeople, Prue and John Quick, at their home 'Sherwood', near Crediton, in mid Devon, Prue showed me a small area in her beautiful garden that she calls her nematon. The garden is entered through arches of naturally forming elder, and inside she showed me an ancient elder that had fallen and regrown many times. There was also hawthorn, oak, silver birch, scots pine, rowan, wild service tree, holly, beech, an ancient apple, hazel and ash growing together naturally on a steep slope. As tempting as it must be for such plantspeople to make a 'garden' within this area, Prue's wish is that it remain a sanctuary for these Celtic trees alone – a memory of when tree spirits were venerated.

Inspiration to plant trees

Trees filter sound, create shade, give habitat and food for birds, insects and animals and provide essential stability for the soil. In the spirit garden, the trees we choose to plant will not only provide joy for generations to come, but can also offer the possibility of a deep contact with an awesome and mysterious energy.

An experience of trees in the wind, their limbs dancing, branches and leaves each demonstrating a different rhythm, observing the differences between the movements in trees, their various sounds, the whistling through the pines, sends us to far-off places in our imagination. From this we can begin to see how choosing trees for the spirit garden is of immense importance.

When planting a new garden, we need to begin by choosing trees that will provide the shelter under which a garden sanctuary may be created. Planting trees will provide protection from the noise of a road and from any potentially undesirable atmospheres from nearby. They will

also protect our smaller plants from the harsh aspects of the weather. Boundaries and enclosures, especially important in the spirit garden, can be created beautifully with the careful planting of the right trees.

I would advise anyone to take a journey to see trees in wild places, or even in town parks. Spend some time sitting with them and watching the movement of those trees that you are drawn to. Return at different times to watch them through the seasons, observe their scent, flowers, form and fruits. Sit with your spine against their trunks. In this way, you will have a chance to rediscover some of the reasons why trees have played such an important part in mythology, and can begin to notice which trees have a positive effect on your emotions and would, therefore, be a good choice to plant in your spirit garden.

Above A myriad of phantasmagorical faces and dreamlike shapes cover the bowl of this mighty 'grandfather' oak tree in Windsor Great Park, on the Surrey/Berkshire borders, where some of England's oldest oaks grow and are protected.

Following pages Sunlight pouring through the firey red leaves of *Acer palmatum* var. *dissectum* in the Savill garden of Windsor Great Park. The delicate tracery of its branches can be seen as a silhouette – the shapes of trees vary enormously and each one of us will experience different feelings and atmospheres around them and under their canopies.

Plants and the Goddess

In many spiritual traditions, the Goddess is responsible for the growth of crops and the flowers of the fields. The worship of the Goddess is growing again all over the world and our own personal celebration of this revival can be expressed by including in our gardens the flowers sacred to the female deities that bring us most inspiration. Plants are frequently named after one of the pantheon of gods and goddesses and, like the iris, this can sometimes be a clue to their subtle significance.

The iris is said to be the eye of the rainbow and a plant whose many-coloured flowers enable us to see the spectrum of colours that make up the universe. In Greek mythology, the winged goddess Iris was the devoted messenger of Zeus and Hera. She travelled the 'rainbow bridge' between heaven and earth in the form of a mortal, and was just as much at home travelling through water as on land.

Many irises do actually have the ability to thrive and bloom in either damp or in dry conditions. Also, they do indeed come in a wide range of colours and they have beautiful winged petals, echoing the form of Iris with her golden wings. If you choose to plant drifts of a range of irises surrounding a seating area in the garden, you will have the opportunity to sit and feel their association with this late spring period of the year, and have a chance to reflect on the reason why this flower is called the iris.

The Christian Virgin Mary is represented by both the red and the white rose, both of them symbolizing pure, spiritual love, and the word 'rosary' is derived from the Latin for rose garden. The Madonna Lily is symbolic of purity and was also made sacred to the Virgin Mary by the Christian Church in the 2nd century.

The winter snowdrop is the flower of the ancient goddess Bride. It blooms in in early February, when she is said to walk the land, as the light returns after winter.

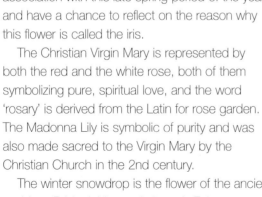

Top right Lilium candidum, sacred to the Virgin Mary. The Greeks and the Romans also associated it with their mother deities, Hera and Juno, and images of the lily can be found on 3000 year-old pottery from the goddess-worshipping culture of ancient Crete.

Below right A perfect red rose with its velvety petals, and on its stems, sharp thorns. The rose is sacred to many esoteric traditions all over the world because of this dual nature, holding the balance of opposites. The red rose was particularly sacred to the mediaeval alchemists and is known as 'The Rose of the Alchemists'.

Far right A deep purple flower of *Iris laevigata*. The iris is known as the flower of light and is the original flower of the heraldic icon Fleur de Lys. To the ancients, the goddess Iris personified the rainbow.

Questing your personal spirit plants

When questing a spirit partnership with a plant, your journey needs to be taken slowly, one step at a time. This gentle quest is more of a 'courtship' of the plant world, and a purpose or an 'intent' needs to be made clear to the spirit world. Your purpose may be to find a plant that will bring healing or emotional support to you at a special time in your life, to bring you lifelong spiritual wisdom, or to bring physical healing to your body in the short term.

Remember, by plants we mean not only flowers, but trees, shrubs, ferns, fruits and vegetables. Remember, too, that as Martín Prechtel says, in questing a personal spirit partnership it is the plant that chooses you, *not* you the plant.

Shamanistic teachings propose that we may have particular plants with which we share a certain 'dream'. If we seriously quest the name of this plant and respectfully learn its gifts, we may also choose to plant it in the garden in a special spot, one that is carefully chosen to amplify its qualities and enable a regular communication.

We can begin by looking for clues to the magical world of plants in the wild landscapes, in our gardens and in the much-loved gardens of well-known gardeners.

Most importantly, however, a request to the spirit world is needed. Maybe a gift will need to be left in the area near where you have been contemplating the plant world. Wherever you find a place you love, take note of the feelings and ambience this creates around you and within you.

Perhaps lie on a moorland bank, surrounded by heather in full bloom, and allow yourself to imagine the plants as beings rather than 'plants'. Remember that you are looking for that invisible dimension, which is mostly hidden until one is completely still and silent.

We may need to contemplate plants at dusk or very early in the morning. These times are points in the day when plants are making vital, but minute, changes, adjusting to the altering light conditions or temperature. They may reveal more of their secrets than when they are at their peak growing time, in full sunlight. Each plant is different, and with time you may begin to sense the best time to sit among particular and much-loved flowers in your garden.

Sometimes, a dream will come to you, in which you may experience a particular plant. When this happens, it is important to try to remember how the plant made you feel in the dream, where it was growing, what you were doing with it and how you were planting it or preparing it. Dreams can be difficult to interpret, but they often hold valuable messages.

Questing Plants for the Spirit Garden

It is considered that most plants love to grow in communities that mirror those where they grow in the wild, and where they will thrive and be far more powerful than if planted alone. This is not always true, however. Some people maintain a beautiful friendship with a lone houseplant that they see everyday and with which they sense a regular, wonderfully blissful energy exchange.

So, if you have a tiny courtyard garden it is fine to choose your own personal spirit plants and place them singly in containers, provided that this is carried out with love and you maintain regular contact with them.

For each of us there are areas of the world where we feel our spirits to be most at home. We may feel a strong resonance with the plants from these places and want to watch them grow in our own gardens in order to evoke the spirit of those places around us.

During the design and creation of gardens, I occasionally dream of a particular plant, which I will then include in the planting scheme of the garden. Invariably, it transpires that this plant is one that is of importance to my client in some way and one which we had not discussed during the initial design brief.

Right Travelling deeply into the flower of the sunny yellow *Sternbergia lutea*. A single stamen appearing as the residing and glowing soul of the flower.

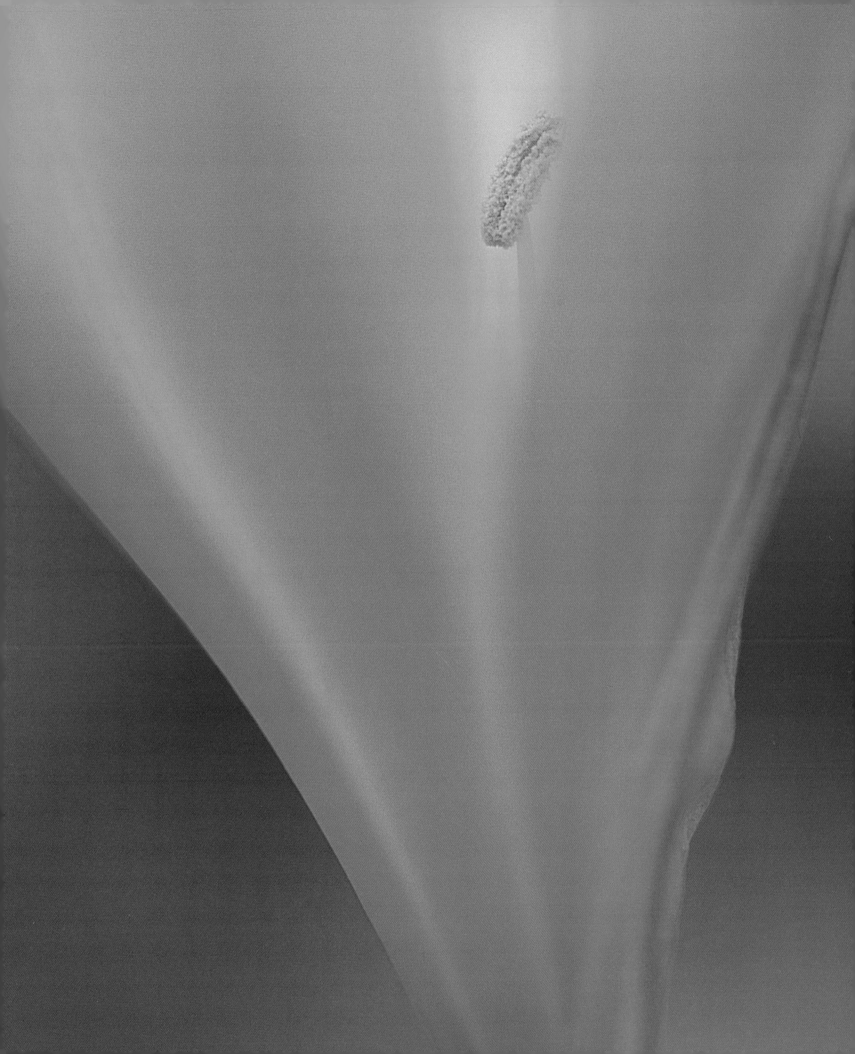

Why not try the following meditation in the quest for a plant to choose you? Set aside some time when you have nothing to do for a few hours, not even gardening. Make a clear intention to contact the spirit world of plants. Travel to a quiet spot outdoors if you can, sit still and preferably on the ground.

Take three, slow, deep breaths and close your eyes.

Feel your next breaths falling deeper into the bottom of your lungs.

Next, breathe into the base of your spine and where your body touches the ground. Imagine yourself walking through an archway of wild shrubs, you find it easy to just stoop gently and pass through.

As you stand up on the other side of the arch, look around you and observe the shape of the landscape you are in, the aromas, the temperature, the plants. Walk for a little while in this place and then find somewhere where you wish to be still.

While you are still, wait awhile and notice what comes to you. When you are ready, walk back through the archway to the place you were sitting, slowly open your eyes and become conscious of your own body again, remembering and maybe writing or drawing what you have seen.

Blessed Be.

During this meditation, you may find that an image of a plant appears. If so, ask the plant what purpose it has in your life. Then carefully and respectfully choose the best way to gracefully embrace this gift in your life. Everyone's experience will be different, there is no measure of success in this adventure, simply a personal, and individual, experience of access to the realities of the plant world.

Sometimes it takes a period of time questing before a plant spirit becomes clear to you. Remember that timing in the world of plants does not follow our own schedules. Like all work in the garden, patience will be required of you.

Whether you are contemplating the power of a single bloom or the family spirit of a whole meadow, bliss is something that so many people have described in these moments. Whether lying under the giant spread of an oak tree, or nose down in the wet mosses around spring primroses, plant size bears no relationship to the emotional charge carried by such moments of contact.

Plants are still the stars of the garden, even in this day of coloured gravel and blue-painted fences. They are the real reason that humans are driven to create gardens. Given the chance, we may allow ourselves to discover the deeper reasons for our gardening obsessions and return to a wiser, more intimate, and childlike relationship with the mysterious world of plants.

Right A blissful, singing, mass of plant spirits in a newly planted seven-acre meadow, created on land near Pulborough, Sussex, England. Part of a long-term project to return the biodiversity of this meadow, it contains a mass of both annual and perennial colour in the form of poppies, corncockles, cornflowers, cornmarigolds and oxe-eye daisies.

The experience of creating our own personal soul garden calls on us to draw deeply from within ourselves, taking time to consider personal needs and choosing inspiration from whatever patterns, plants and stories of the spirit that we are drawn to.

Going deeper

Designing a sacred garden

Creating a home for the soul is probably the unconscious intention of all passionate gardeners and garden designers. I feel that home is something we all seek, for as the saying goes, home is where the heart is.

Most of us feel uprooted and dispossessed in some way. We move from place to place, with few of us having lived in one home all our lives, and even those who have seem to have lost their spiritual relationship with the land. Making a garden can begin the process of recovering from our inner sense of homelessness.

For the artist and landscape designer, Topher Delaney, her first task with a client is evoking their social, spiritual and physical personal terrain. She says we are all spiritual immigrants, looking for the Promised Land. Her intention is to interpret this sacred landscape and bring it into form.

She first asks her clients about their memories before the age of seven, and uses these as the basis for her garden design. As in my own work, she attempts to represent the inner, imaginary and spiritual world of her clients.

From the information given, Topher creates a picture that will precede the making of her bold and individualistic contemporary gardens. When creating Paul Gupta's garden in California, USA, she asked him to describe memories of his childhood garden in Delhi, India, and she even drew inspiration from the collections of his spontaneous scribblings made during the period of investigating the brief.

The image of Paul's garden shown here is Topher's representation of his memories of the colours of India. They are chosen from the colours of Indian fabrics, and painted on beautiful, curving walls that form the structure of what she refers to as both a sensual and pictorial garden, one in which an inner sense of being at home can be felt.

Paul says the garden is a creation of his own familiar paradise and is able to transport him to a sacred space that inspires him in his work.

Right A brazier containing a fire that lights up the brightly painted walls of Topher Delaney's garden for Paul Gupta in California.

Working organically and with the cycles of nature

For me, a most powerful way of feeling at home is by growing food for myself and my family. This work takes me to my allotment, where I grow vegetables and fruit organically. The plot is no immaculate piece of ground nor a beautifully styled potager – I am too busy to be able to boast that!

When I visit my allotment, I know that the weeds are growing faster than my crops, but despite this, my often random and experimental efforts to grow food continue to be deeply satisfying.

It is true that the soil there is far better than the clay soil of my own garden, but something else was driving me to do the apparently impossible, and one day I began to realize what it was.

I began to see that the act of growing food to eat is as sacred – if not more so – as creating a visually beautiful garden. I'm sure this is not new information to many kitchen gardeners, but I had to find it out for myself.

This experience has brought another layer of a primal relationship with the land. As I began to see that the flavour of my vegetables directly relates not only to my personal treatment of the soil, but also to variations in the year's weather and the number of slugs around that year, sometimes it all felt completely out of my hands; at other times, I know I am making a difference by my work.

The results are in the flavours on the plate, and I have developed a heightened sense of the importance of my food to my well-being. I used not to be a keen cook, so it has come as a surprise to discover a new-found passion for cooking with my home-grown produce. I can't wait to get back from the allotment with a handful of exquisitely tasty globe artichokes, or of the few carrots that have managed to push past the weeds, resist carrot fly and a lack of watering.

For me, the embarrassment of my less-than-perfect vegetable plot is made up for by the sensuality and sacredness that result from cropping, carefully preparing and, of course, eating, the food I have grown with my own hands.

The magic of making compost – becoming aware of the cycle of life

I have found that composting materials for the vegetable garden can become an equally passionate exercise, as more and more waste items from my lifestyle are discovered to be possible additions, from weeds, grass cuttings, shredded newspaper and vegetable peelings.

The important point I want to make about this process of recycling is that it gives the gardener a hands-on experience of the cycle of life and renewal. As the waste breaks down through the action of microbes, it naturally transforms into a life-giving substance that encourages our food to grow healthily, and hence contributes to the life of our bodies.

No costly outlay is needed to experience this magical process of garden alchemy, one that turns plant and other suitable waste into gold for the garden. To begin, all you need is plenty of enthusiasm and a little spare wood or straw bales to build a container.

The organisms needed to ensure the transformation of waste into rich, nourishing food for our crops are ever-present in the soil. The organic gardener, who only uses natural composts, and who gardens without using any slug pellets or chemicals to kill insects or microbes, is able to rest at ease, knowing that the food grown is as uncontaminated as possible, a luxury, indeed, in these times.

This experience brings the gardener into personal contact with both the workings of the natural cycles of life in the garden, and those cycles operating on the planet as a whole. Such contact helps to show us how we are an active part of the cycle of nature.

Physical and spiritual nourishment are undoubtedly connected and are brought alive in the experience of growing food. For me, an experience of being at home on the land has also been found in the place where I grow my food.

Right A handful of bulbs showing the exquisite colours of their skins. One of the gardener's privileges is the observation of the beauty of seeds, corms and bulbs, and their diverse and intriguing forms, scents, textures and colours.

Sourcing materials for the sacred garden

Top right A collection of found objects from the beaches around Derek Jarman's home in Kent, England. Each piece was thoughtfully collected and added to the garden of *Crambe maritima* and scarlet poppies.

Far right An outdoor altar in Derek Jarman's garden on which he displayed an ever-changing collection of natural and man-made found objects. Metal, wood, shells, stones and even plastic objects, transformed by the sea and the sun, were put here on view, as a tribute to nature's reclamation of them.

Going deeper may involve going back to our primal dream landscape, whether it is through our childhood experiences or by the act of growing food. When thinking about designing a sacred garden, however, we also need to remember that all the materials that are used in its making are of significance.

Working with the materials of the earth

By this, I mean that choosing timbers that have been felled from a wild rainforest to make a deck or a table and chairs, or using limestone from a threatened habitat, would bring an uncomfortable lack of care and integrity to any garden space. In my opinion, this in itself would render the garden less than sacred.

There are many wood sources today that are guaranteed to originate from renewable forests.

Some companies that deal in wood pride themselves not just on the quality of what they remove, but in what they give back to the communities with which they work (see Resources on page 130).

Take care to investigate the source of all the materials you use and the way in which they have been processed, for both will have an effect on the atmosphere in your garden and on your conscious relationship to it.

For instance, the contents of a commercially available bag of compost may prove to be mainly peat dug up from wild habitats in Eastern Europe or Southern Ireland. Could we feel easy knowing this, and would it be suitable for the sacred garden, where we are seeking to find a sense of spiritual harmony, and where a balance and connection with the natural places of the world is a vital element?

So how can we approach this difficult area of care in sourcing materials at a time when our shops are full of enticing items from all over the world? We can start by asking questions of the suppliers. We may then decide to go further and to investigate the source of the product with the actual manufacturers.

Many manufacturers acknowledge the growing concerns people have about the origin of all sorts of products, and often they will be able to give you precise information about where, how and from what their goods are made.

This begins an approach to our lives that may lead to a developing discernment. It is an approach that may become a part of your way of life and one which includes getting choosy about almost everything.

Such an approach introduces what is known as Deep Ecology into our lives. This means that we make a difference to the world we live in by considering all of our actions. This process is a measure of the commitment that we have to the garden itself and to the world of nature beyond.

The spirit of materials and objects

Creating a sacred space demands that we know all the different pieces that contribute to it as a whole. The more knowledge we have of them, the clearer their relationship is with the space, and this further increases the garden's capacity to make us feel truly at home, and to bring us an experience of the spirit.

Filling a garden with items we love assures the development of a rich and personal sacred space. The items chosen may include plants from places we have visited that bring us good memories, pebbles and shells found in a spot where we experienced a certain joy, for example, or an insight into the magic of a particular landscape.

The inclusion of metal items can represent to us the power of fire to transform. The inclusion of a place for lighting a fire brings the possibility of light and warmth at night, but also the opportunity to include the energy of the sun, in the form of wood transformed into ashes and added to the soil.

If it is possible to include some items that have been made by hand, and particularly by our own hands, then all the better. Making an item by hand imbues it with all the positive feelings, thoughts and even prayers we held at the time in which we made it. The placement of such a piece of work brings this energy to the garden. Creating a special place for this work to be sited in in the garden – a shrine, a niche or even just a spot that you are particularly fond of – empowers the feelings even further, bringing a deep and very personal atmosphere to the whole space.

Remember that a garden can be a stage for the beauty of nature as we experience her in the wild as well as in a cultivated setting. All the textures, forms and colours in the wood, stone and plants of the garden can serve to excite us and to invoke deep feelings within us. Familiarity with their origins brings the presence of these places with them and further enriches the garden where they are sited.

Creating our own rituals in the sacred garden

Ritual can be described as simply a symbolic act that focuses our attention on a particular intention. American teacher, author and mythology expert, Joseph Campbell (1904–87), in his book *Myths to Live By*, said that ritual gives form and depth to human life, bringing significant markers to the important events in our lives.

The act of making food can be joyful and ritualistic, or it can be unconscious and careless. Birthdays and Christmas celebrations are traditional, conscious rituals with which many of us are familiar, but there are also deeper and much more personal experiences of ritual available to us that we can develop and make a space for in the sacred garden.

Looking once again to the ancient, sacred places of the world, we can find evidence of simple rituals designed to offer gifts and prayers to the spirits in the powerful places in nature. An example of such places are the holy wells found in Ireland and Cornwall, such as the one at Modran, Cornwall, England.

At these wells clooties, an Irish word for pieces of fabric taken from clothing, are tied to nearby trees. The knot marks the connection between the human and the spirit world. Prayers are sent through the pieces of clothing, which are permeated with the life of the wearer, and these prayers are blown to the spirit world as the wind moves through them.

This is a truly simple and personal ritual that draws on the power of a sacred place, which in turn is empowered by a history of visitors through time. I use this as an example of a ritual because of its simplicity. It shows how easily our own rituals can be created and carried out in our own outdoor sacred spaces.

On a more communal level, in Derbyshire, England, we still see well dressings, a pagan way of making thanksgiving offerings to the spirits of the village well. Clearly, the village well, long before the advent of national water supplies, brought an

invaluable source of water, but some wells were also seen as sacred in themselves, and many of them are places said to be associated with the goddess Brighde.

Well dressings are exquisite designs, made completely with flowers, and they express the village heart. They are still created today and, understandably, attract much attention because of their colour and finely designed structures.

This ancient ritual can inspire us to create our own rituals in the garden, perhaps one made with the flowers that we have grown ourselves, so as to lend more beauty and significance to the offering. Our gardens, when tended with love and care, will bring an abundance of materials for the making of gifts – flowers, seed heads and seeds, leaves and wood.

A simple altar in the garden can provide a focus for personal rituals.

Top right Sharon Osmund's garden in Berkeley, California, USA, where a Goddess figure against a tree trunk is surrounded by lush green foliage.

Far right In the garden of John Glover a simple candle burns in an old terracotta pot, lighting up a carved Buddha that sits surrounded by an aura of green hop and ivy leaves.

The garden at night

Let us forget expensive, electrical garden lighting techniques in the sacred garden, for the stars, the night sky and the moonlight are all we need. Solar-powered little lights can be used to illuminate essential steps to the house if need be, but by switching off all the house lights, stepping outside and allowing ourselves to experience the night sky in all its purity, we can experience nature's beauty, secrets and cycles.

The making of gardens with night-time in mind is rarely spoken of, but to me one of the most magical times in the garden is when I step outside to have a peek at the garden under the night sky, just before going to bed. The garden seems to be drawing me outside and encouraging me to stay, although I might feel cold and in need of sleep. I might even feel a little nervous of the darkness and wonder where to place each footstep, but both the stars and the silence seduce me into wandering.

Moonlight bathes the garden in a light that brings into view particular plants and structures, covering them with an ethereal silvery glow. As Derek Jarman said, the garden seems to dissolve in the darkness.

I have designed many gardens to be walked in under the light of the Moon and to celebrate the Goddess. The reflection of moonlight in water and on plants, whereby plants seem to exude more light from their leaves and flowers than they receive, are two natural phenomena that a designer will love to use in the creation of a garden.

There are a whole array of plants that have silvery leaves. Most of these love the sunlight and require an open, sunny position to grow in, otherwise they lose their natural glow. Such a position in the garden will also place them correctly for exposure to the rays of the Moon.

Personal favourite symbols and glyphs can be brought to life at night if their shapes are planted out as little hedges using, for example, santolina or lavender. A spiral of cotton lavender or a Celtic knot planted in dwarf lavender are equally simple to create.

Extensive parterres can be made to hold an array of plants, and the 'negative' space within the clipped box hedge filled with silver-leaved plants, such as artemisia or white-flowering marguerites. Other suitable plants can be used to 'paint' an image or shape that can be viewed under the light of the Moon.

Many herbs have silvery coloured leaves, such as wormwood and sage. A whole garden of healing herbs can often reflect a mass of moonlight, and a surrounding hedge of clipped *Santolina* will bring even more definition to its form.

As the Moon waxes and wanes from new, to full, to old, her full glory can be experienced directly in the garden. The triple aspects of the Goddess, from Maiden, to Mother, to Crone, are all mirrored in the cycles of the Moon's movement. The Maiden is represented by the new, the full is akin to the Mother, and the waning is associated with the Crone.

The Moon draws tides, measures time and influences the water in our own bodies; indeed, we are said to be made up of 80 per cent water. Experiencing the differences felt in our bodies and in our dreams when the Moon is in a different phase is a possibility for all of us. Even when the moon can't be seen, it is still working its magic. The moon's cycle of movement and its reflection of light from the sun is a primary influence on the evolution of humans. We have been referred to as 'lunar primates' because we are the only animals whose female cycle of fertility is controlled by the monthly cycle of the moon instead of the sun.

The moon also has less physical affects on our lives, influencing our dreams and emotions. Sitting in the garden and feeling the journey of the moon and the stars across the sky, month to month and through the year, can bring us into a relationship with the bigger universe. It will also encourage the contemplation of ourselves within it.

Right The full moon over trees lighting up the night sky, a sight which reminds us that we too are living on a planet which is always moving in a continuous cycle. When we slow down enough to feel the moon's changes we can become aware of the fluctuations in our moods and even the feelings in our bodies as the moon waxes and wanes. Our gardens can be a lovely place in which to experience lunar magic.

Silvery leaved plants that reflect moonlight

Cotton lavender (*Santolina chamaecyparissus*)
Lavender (*Lavandula*) varieties – some are more
silvery than others
Betony (*Stachys lanata*)
Sage (*Salvia lavandulifolia*)
Honeybush (*Melianthus major*)
Wormwood (*Artemisia* 'Powis Castle')
Pearl everlasting (*Anaphalis margaritacea*)
Wormwood (*Artemisia ludoviciana* 'Valerie Finnis')
Helichrysum italicum
Sea holly (*Eryngium giganteum* 'Miss
Willmott's Ghost')
Cardoon (*Cynara cardunculus*)
Fuchsia magellanica var. *gracilis* 'Variegata'
Convolvulus cneorum
Senecio greyi
Elaeagnus angustifolia
Bramble (*Rubus thibetanus*), if you don't mind
the spines
Pear (*Pyrus salicifolia* 'Pendula')
Gum tree (*Eucalyptus niphophila*)
Birch (*Betula*), *B. pendula* varieties and *B. utilis* var.
jacquemontii have very white trunks

White flowers that also glow under moonlight, in the half light and even when there is no moon

Tobacco plant (*Nicotiana*)
Rose (*Rosa*), 'Iceberg' standards particularly, which
give a height to the reflection
Madonna lily (*Lilium candidum*)

Night-time fragranced plants

Tobacco plant (*Nicotiana*)
Honeysuckle (*Lonicera*)
Jasmine (*Jasminum*)
Roses (*Rosa*)

The sacred cycle of life, the sun and the earth

The cycle of the seasons is ever-present in our gardens, a reminder of both our mortality and of our connection to nature. Every ancient culture made ritual and celebratory acknowledgement of the passing of the seasons and of the gifts brought to us by nature.

The American Jungian analyst, storyteller and author, Clarissa Pinkola Estes, who wrote *Women Who Run With the Wolves*, talks about the life-death-life cycle. She says we are always changing, growing, shifting and shedding, just as nature itself. We need to be able to accept this and to dance with it in our relationships, thereby understanding ourselves as creatures inextricably linked to the rhythms of the planet Earth.

An especial awareness of the death aspect of life is important. The darkness of winter is related to the times in our lives when we are ending something, or maybe gestating, like a seed buried deep in the earth – nature being experienced as 'dying back' before new life can commence.

Our gardens have much to teach us about the seasons. Like the movement of the Moon, the planetary cyclic movements bring the seasonal changes. The spring and autumn equinoxes mark the time when the sun crosses the equator, making the night equal in length to the day.

The Celtic Fire Festivals of Britain – the returning of the light

The summer and winter solstices occur when the sun reaches its maximum distance from the equator and mark a turning point in the seasons. The summer solstice occurs when the sun touches the tropic of Cancer, around 21st June, and the winter solstice when it touches that of Capricorn, around 21st December.

These dates, together with the so-called 'cross-quarter' dates, mark the Celtic Fire festivals of Britain. These 'cross-quarter' dates are Imbolc, falling halfway between the winter solstice and the spring equinox; Beltane, falling halfway between the spring equinox and the summer solstice; Lammas, falling halfway between the summer solstice and the autumn equinox, and Samhain (Halloween), falling halfway between the autumn equinox and the winter solstice.

As gardeners, becoming aware of these special times – their affect on the amount of light reaching the land, their historical significance and meaning to our ancestors – brings a new spiritual awareness of life on the land. Celebrating these times increases our sense of connection with the subtle, but significant, shifts of the seasons and allows us to contemplate these shifts as mirrors of our own inner rhythms.

At one of the coldest, and often most depressing, times of the year, the spring Celtic Fire Festival, Imbolc, is said to represent the time when the light 'returns'. to the Earth and it can, indeed, be felt as a gentle shift in the natural world.

Right The lighting of ceremonial fires used to be one part of the marking of the seasonal progressions in Britain.

Far right At Walsingham Abbey in Norfolk, England, site of Christian pilgrimages even today, and of an an ancient holy well, a carpet of snowdrops covers the woodland floor.

The goddess Bride was said to travel across the landscape on this night, visiting people's homes and bringing them blessings. Gifts were left out for her beside the family hearth and the family would pray for her to visit them and receive their gifts, in exchange for her blessings on their lives.

Bride is the ancient Celtic goddess of the land and when Christianity arrived the Celts continued to worship her under the new name of Mary.

Bride is also known as the Goddess of the Hearth, both at home and in the smithy. Bride inspires the writing of poetry and is the deity said to assist women in childbirth. She is a 'triple' fire goddess, with Brighde – her Irish name – meaning 'bright arrow',

I have noticed that on the day of Imbolc in dull February, small signs of change can be seen in the quality of the light. There are also other signs; a Little Owl calls as its mate returns, and the opening of snowdrops begins. Indeed, the snowdrop is the flower said to be sacred to Bride; she is known as the Snowdrop Queen.

This is often a hard time of the year for people in the Northern Hemisphere, as there has now been a considerable period of time with dull weather, shorter days and little sunshine. Getting dressed-up and going out into the cold winter garden to catch the sun whenever it comes out is one way of getting the light we need and avoiding depression. Noticing the gently, but definitely returning light, from the time of Imbolc, has helped me survive the length of the English winter by making me conscious of the ever-changing cycle of the seasons.

The coming of spring

Spring is the celebration of new life and renewal, with the spring equinox coming around 21st March. At this time, the Greek goddess Demeter was said to have found her daughter Persephone, after a winter of grieving and searching for her.

Demeter's joy is said to be seen on Earth in the form of blessings that she poured upon the land, bringing seeds to germinate and creating new life again. The life-death-life cycle in the garden has fully shifted into its life phase. Something has returned and we can begin to feel like Demeter. We feel like waking up and beginning new projects, especially in the garden.

This is the time that we will have to work hard to keep up with the sudden acceleration of growth in the garden. We take on an obsessive mood; planting seeds, clearing beds of winter debris and watching in awe the delightful, gentle unfolding of waking spring flowers, such as daffodils, primroses and bluebells. We set about madly implementing the wild and ambitious projects that we have dreamed of during the winter, in an armchair next to the fireplace!

By the time 1st May has arrived, everything is in full swing, ready for the celebration of May Day, or Beltane. In times gone by Beltane Eve was the most riotous and outrageous celebration of the year, when people courted the god Pan in order to bring both a fertile harvest, and a fruitful crop of babies the next year. 'Into the woods!', was the call, and a wild celebration of fertility was encouraged.

In Ireland, it was traditional to decorate trees and bushes for this festival, and all over Europe a popular ritual was to jump over the fire with someone whom you loved enough to spend the following year with.

Gardens are burgeoning now, as is the whole of nature. Why not celebrate by lighting a Beltane fire in the garden and drink to the fullness of your life, thank the spirits for the ones you love and call for blessings on your relationships.

Top right The unfurling first leaf of a germinating seed in the damp earth.

Far right A sea of purple, mauve and white crocuses bursting through the lawn in late winter and marking the coming of spring. Their purity and simplicity seem to bring fresh hope for the new year of growth in the garden and a taste of the colour of the flowers to come.

Summer solstice and the harvest festival

Summer is the high time of growth. The Earth has reached the mid-point on her journey around the sun, and although it is hard to believe at this moment, from now on the days will become shorter as the wheel of time turns towards winter.

Midsummer is said to be the time when matters of love are in the air; roses are blooming and the scents at night are heady. The summer solstice is a magical time for making wishes, so why not invent a ritual that includes a wish, perhaps with a posy gathered from the rich flowers in your garden – especially roses, which are sacred to the Goddess.

If your personal spirit garden includes water somewhere, why not write a piece of poetry for this night and speak it into the waters; place petals on its surface, thank the spirits and call for what you desire. Water is the element sacred to the Greek goddess Aphrodite and to the Celtic Rhiannon, both of whom were born from the sea, the ocean of emotion.

By the time we reach 1st August, known to the Celts as Lammas, and more familiar to us as the beginning of the harvest-festival season, we are becoming aware of little changes in the garden. Many of the herbaceous flowers and flowering shrubs will be beginning to fade, unless, of course, we have been clever and included such later beauties as *Eucryphia* x *nymansensis*, dahlias, cosmos, verbena, *Ceratostigma willmottianum* and repeat flowering roses, such as 'Iceberg'.

I always feel a beautiful sense of peace at this time of year, when the race to grow seems to have subsided, the robin's call changes and just a sprinkling of later flowers grace the garden. From now on, the light begins slowly to change and becomes soft and silvery as the autumn equinox approaches.

Lammas precedes autumn and marks the appearance of fruits and vegetables, corn and beans. Harvest-festival celebrations traditionally fall between Lammas and the autumn equinox.

Right Midsummer in the garden at Sticky Wicket in Dorset, England. It is rich with flowers such as *Allium sphaerocephalon*, *Phlox paniculata* 'Franz Schubert', and oreganom. Here the flowers are show no sign of declining and the heady mix of scents sends us swooning. Lying among the flowers at the time when the earth has reached the mid-point of her journey around the sun can be a conscious celebration of the abundance in your garden and your life.

Autumn equinox and winter

According to the Celtic calendar, the year ends at Samhain, 31st October, popularly known today as Halloween. Much fun is made on this special night, especially with the newer tradition of trick or treat.

Right around the world this has always been the time when the veil between the spirit and the physical worlds was said to be 'thinner' than usual and we could take the opportunity to make contact with the spirit worlds and, in particular, to speak to loved ones who have passed away. At this time of year, too (1st November), the Mexicans celebrate the Feast of the Dead and acknowledge their ancestors in many colourful and playful rituals.

Hecate is the Greek goddess of this season, as is Kali, from the continent of India. Both are goddesses associated with death and transformation and their images are sometimes uncomfortable to us, just as is the thought of the approaching winter. In this seaon, death is the corresponding point on the wheel of life. In the garden, the frosts have usually started by now and the tender plants are withering or being brought into the greenhouse for protection from the cold.

The first strong winds begin to strip the leaves from the trees, leaving their bare outlines ready to receive the frosts of winter. Their sap flow has slowed, dormancy has begun and their seeds have been shed. Yet the buds ready for the spring are miraculously in evidence on plants such as rhododendrons, magnolias and camellias. These little buds are covered with protective layers of fleshy scales that will guard them from the cold of the winter months.

Only a few weeks later, on 21st December, the Earth will reach its furthest point from the sun, and the winter equinox will arrive. For the Celts, this was the time when the sun was held magically within the stored seeds, corms and bulbs. The seeds held the energy of the sun locked up during their dormancy through the months of cold and

rain, sometimes needing to be kept in the dark, but certainly needing to rest before the new growth period began.

Christmas is the Christian celebration most closely linked to the Celtic winter equinox of the 21st December. The return of the sun king was celebrated in pre-Christian times and represented in the celebration at this time, as the sun began to sail closer to the earth.

So, even when we think that we are in the middle of winter, the light has begun gradually to change. There seems to be no point of absolute stillness, except perhaps at the exact moment of the winter equinox, when the sun is furthest away from the earth

From now, right on through the winter, our gardens lie sleeping, like the child in its crib. Frost, ice and snow may cover its surfaces, and sometimes something precious dies in the cold. Mostly, we await the return of life and of growth, with the dream of our garden held firmly in our imagination and memories during the long winter nights, and with plans for its further enrichment in the spring hatching.

Lighting a fire, inside the home or outside in the garden, honours the ancient tradition of celebrating the Goddess of the Flame, Hestia. In this time of darkness and cold, the sun is, in fact, starting day-by-day to come closer to us, as we once again, slowly and sleepily, return to the time of the snowdrops.

Top right Pumpkins cut out with candles placed inside them – a familiar and slightly humorous Halloween tradition, deriving from the ancient time when the spirits of the dead were acknowledged at this time when the 'veil between the worlds is thin'.

Far right The fruits of the earth are now changing, mushrooms appear in their many and multi-coloured forms. Here the red leaves of acers decorate the ground where bracket fungi and toadstools grow.

Following pages The herb garden at Wisley, Surrey, England in midwinter, covered in hoar frost. The atmosphere here is one of stillness, growth being held at bay by the low temperatures and lack of sunlight. But even in the heavy sleep of winter, the fire of last summer's sunshine is being held, although dormant, in the seeds of the plants, in the tubers, bulbs and roots and in the sap of the trees.

Gardens as personal spaces for spiritual practice

The garden can provide a most beautiful, peaceful and inspirational space for most spiritual practices. Deidre Gough, an alternative therapy masseuse and psychotherapist, wanted to develop her small courtyard garden in London, England. Her garden designer, Kristina Fitzsimmons, originally designed a garden that included decking, a hot tub, a water feature and a rill.

When Deirdre saw Christine's designs, she began to see the potential for a sacred garden, and the two of them collaborated further to develop an enclosed sanctuary space for personal relaxation and meditation.

Deirdre also wanted to include in the garden aspects of her spiritual work and they created what she calls a 'tantric garden', which includes representations of the chakras, the Indian term for describing the energy centres of the physical and etheric body.

Visual and energetic tantric elements were introduced into the garden in the form of the main ornamental features. A sculpture of a male torso with water trickling down the spine, then travelling along a rill and down into a bubble water feature marks the circulation of both physical and spiritual energy within the body.

Open areas in a garden can be created to provide a space for movement work, such as *t'ai chi* or dance. For one client, I created a garden with a central lawned area to be used for dance workshops. Planted areas around the grass were designed to represent the elements of earth, fire, air and water, forming a focus for the dance.

A peaceful and tranquil garden is, of course, the most natural place for meditation and contemplation. A sacred garden needs the careful placement of seating areas in secluded places, where you will feel relaxed and not exposed to view. A sheltered place, one that gives us protection from the elements and yet allows us to be touched by them, enables a depth of experience in meditation that is brought about by the meeting of our inner world and the world of nature.

Creating a garden in a minimalist style, perhaps inspired by the deliberate simplicity of the Zen gardens of Japan, may provide the right style of meditative environment for someone wishing to achieve that sublime state of 'no thing'.

A more lush and leafy place may be needed for those wishing to contemplate the richness of nature as a route to enlightenment. Those exploring the secrets of the world of shamanism, may need a garden with many little nooks and crannies, trees and rocks, places for the lighting of fires and leaving gifts to the spirits.

The Buddhist walking meditations are ideally practised in a peaceful garden, but where the busy sounds of people and cars are heard in the garden space, those practising meditation are always encouraged to include these sounds, rather than seeking another, more perfect, spot.

When designing your sacred garden, remember to consider your own personal spiritual practice and what you need to carry this out. Think about how much privacy you would like and consider carefully which part of the garden is most suited for these needs.

Top right Deirdre Gough's garden, which provides a sacred space for meditation and contemplation and a reflection on her own spiritual tantric work with the chakras.

Far right A pair of sculptures on a stream bank in the Gardens of Gaia, Cranbrook, Kent, England. Placed under the trees among cow parsley and wild garlic, they complement this peaceful and tranquil garden space, a perfect place for the contemplation of wildness.

Public gardens

Soil scientists were brought in to transform the waste materials from the site into the soils needed. Architects and designers were encouraged to draw on futuristic visions to produce spaces that are highly energy efficient and provide an intensive care unit for plants from all over the world.

The result is series of architecturally beautiful domes that merge into the surrounding landscape and house plants from the humid tropics, warm temperate and temperate regions of the world.

Tim Smit, whose vision has driven the Eden Project, began this work after restoring the Lost Gardens of Heligan. His work seems to be lead by his desire to return a vision of nature and human creativity to an age that appears to have lost its way. He says he will try almost anything to get over the message of interdependance between ourselves and the plant world.

As a result of this vision, the Eden Project is no tree museum – the pods contain multi-level landscapes that include beautiful displays of all kinds of plants from the different regions of the world. Interpretation methods are innovative and are not shy in expressing Tim's vision; exhibitions from artists, designers and sculptors are an important part of this approach.

The Eden Project wants to touch the heart of all those who visit it and it aims to show just how connected we all are with nature. The Project offers a chance not only to see, but to feel the beauty and complexity of our own planet and how it provides us with all our day-to-day needs, as well as with the stage for all the stories and myths of our inner lives.

By complete contrast to the intimate, private gardens created by individuals, there are public spaces that are designed to bring about a deep experience of being in nature, more so than traditional parks, familiar to most towns and cities. Such spaces are designed to give the visitor an intimate experience of nature and spirit.

The Eden Project

To my mind, the Eden Project, often called a modern-day wonder of the world, is a most soulful garden – by name of, course, but mainly by its intention to show our exciting interdependence with plants, and its drive to engage everyone, whether or not they have any interest in plants.

The structure and innovation of this project is immensely exciting. The Eden project has been built on the site of a disused clay pit, Bodelva, near St. Austell in Cornwall, England. Massive, interconnecting geodesic 'pods' have been built, with plastic hexagons built into the rockface to retain the heat of the sun and provide the height needed for the huge tropical trees.

Esalen Gardens

In Big Sur, California, USA, the gardens of The Esalen Institute are built in a place once sacred to the Esselen Indians. The Institute is a well-known educational and retreat centre that brings together some of the most renowned philosophers, artists and thinkers from all over the world.

Above The tropical biome at the Eden Project. The beginnings of lush rainforest growth are in evidence and eventually there will be towering rainforest trees reaching the geodesic rooftops and creating, like no other artificial biome in the world, a sensation of being in the forest itself.

Right In the temperate biome of the Eden Project the uniquely designed interconnecting hexagons provide a science fiction look to what is the largest conservatory in the world.

Given the spiritual focus of the Institute, the gardens have been primarily designed to provide the visitor with a profoundly sacred perspective. The gardens are a true celebration of the beauty and drama of nature and are said to bring about soul renewal and a restoration of vitality.

There are hot springs, breathtaking views over the ocean and a rocky ledge where rushing river waters meet the ocean. This is thought to have been where the Indians had their sweat lodges, used for ritual purification. Today, a redwood meditation house sits close to this sacred site.

Esalen gardens have been carefully developed on a spiritually significant site of natural beauty and ancient history. They can, therefore, impart great joy, a sense of wholeness and the spiritual heritage of the landscape.

Les Jardins de l'Imaginaire

The sensitive, modern designs of Kathryn Gustafson have produced Les Jardins de l'Imaginaire – 'The Gardens of the Imagination'. They are on a wooded slope above the small, rural French town of Terrasson-la-Villedieu.

The garden is a guided journey through a series of ideas about life. An area known as the Sacred Wood, for example, symbolizes the Romans' ideas about the relationship between spirit and nature. Another area demonstrates the systematic approach taken by monks in the use of plants, and a huge, metal trelliswork structure is planted up with a mass of climbing roses. Kathryn refers to this as 'Lipstick Alley'!

The garden contains modern-day symbols, such as golden ribbons threaded through trees to represent the bumpy periods of life. It ends with stone panels engraved with representations of the courses of the world's five great rivers.

When speaking of this public and rural garden, Kathryn says the public need know nothing of its conceptual content, but hopefully, in their own way, they will feel its emotion.

The spirit in the garden of life

Gardens are indeed sacred spaces, from birth right through life and in the places of transition, the 'little deaths' in between. I can remember all of the gardens in my life and each of them has meaning, relating to my spiritual growth at that time.

The ancients made sacred places, such as the burial chamber at Newgrange in Ireland, not only to mark a life, but to assist and honour the passing on of the human spirit into the afterlife. 'Good' grieving in many traditional societies is considered essential for the spirits to move on into the afterlife, and without it we are left with restless spirits around us.

In Stockholm's Woodland Cemetery, developed between 1915 and 1940, Swedish architects, Erik Gunner Asplund and Sigurd Lewerentz, evolved a new kind of cemetery,
one of 'communal remembrance'. Although the cemetery included ancient symbolic and traditional influences, the design wasn't ruled by them.
The landscape slowly evolved, allowing the visitor to include and create their own rituals, and it purposefully aimed to re-integrate death and life in this beautiful and profound creation.

Erik and Sigurd recognized the ancient significance of the *locus sacer*, the sacred place, and by taking as their starting point the beauty and character of the area's natural terrain – earth and sky, forest and clearing, meadow and marsh – and introducing modernist building and landscape design of the time, they successfully worked to enhance the natural power of this woodland.

The Woodland Cemetery landscape is designed to be sensed rather than viewed; associations with death and re-birth have been evoked and a landscape with a universal sense of the spirit has been created.

Visiting a wilderness such as the uplifting woodland landscape around the Kennebec river, Maine, USA, home to moose and bear, can open us to our deeper inner lives, and bring us a little closer to our soul upon our return.

Right The autumn colours of New England are characterised by their mix of evergreen and deciduous trees. The river-washed stones will be different every year, being driven downstream to a new place as the water travels to the ocean.

Creating a garden for the soul

Adrienne Lorkin's great passion in life is climbing mountains. When I first met her she told me how much she loved making the descent from the heights of the South American peaks into the lush, tropical valleys below. This was the landscape of her dreams and the one that was to become the inspiration for her own spirit garden.

Through her 'hands-on' making of her own sacred garden – instead of simply handing over all of the responsibility to a contractor – through the adventure of tracking down each of the individual plants on the plan and then personally settling every one into the ground, she not only realized a dream, but also came out of a period of illness and back to full health.

The 'little deaths' we experience throughout our lives bring forward new life, this is what we see every year in the garden and what we are given the privilege of learning about, thereby going on to be able co-create with nature. Adrienne felt that she was creating her own soul home, while healing her body during the process, and that her spirit had been implanted in the garden during her lifetime. The seeds for this had always been there and the alchemical recipe for its germination lay in her own hands.

The landscape which inspired a transformation in me – Uluru in the Australian outback – is also one that is fundamental to the the spiritual beliefs of the Aranda and Loritja tribes of Australian Aborigines. They believe in a profound relationship with life and death in the landscape and, indeed, this forms the basis for their whole belief system.

Professer T.G. Strehlow, the writer and academic who spent the majority of his life in Central Australia, in his great work *Songs of Central Australia*, speaks of the Aborigines' 'sacred earth site' or everlasting home, known as *Pmara Kutata*. This earth site, which is made up of mountains, waterholes, springs and creeks, is the place that holds all the ancestors from whom every Aborigine is descended.

All the ancient stories of the lives and deeds of the immortal beings in Aborigine mythology are recorded in this landscape, in fact the whole landscape is the physical embodiment of their living, ancient, family tree. Even the stories of the land's creation are encoded in the land itself, and include past incarnations of the self – sometimes in the form of their own totemic animals. Therefore the land even holds the stories of their own role in its creation.

How would our lives be if we, too, were to develop such a close relationship to our landscapes? The spiritual and physical healing nature of plants and the garden has been often spoken of in this book, though above all, the making of a garden has been seen as an opportunity to enter into an intense and lasting relationship with nature.

It is hard for us, as members of the modern world, who have lost our way on the earth we tread upon, to know how, and even where, we belong. I myself had to travel a great distance to experience my own soul landscape. Sometimes our soul landscape may be held in a childhood memory, a landscape that for one reason or another can never be revisited. Some of us may never encounter our soul landscape in the real world, but it can be enough to find it in our memories and dreams. An 'imaginary' landscape can be just as viable as an inspiration for a sacred garden as a real landscape.

In the end we can be seen to be simply creating a home for the soul, where the life-death-life cycle can be played out, where the alchemical process of transformation can be seen to be operating right under our feet and where our inner and outer landscapes can take form.

Gardens are gifts to the spirits and they can, if we allow it, be prayers from the heart. Whenever we work in the garden, or create something beautiful, we can make this our song to the earth and a call for home.

Right A path through a garden of ferns in the Lost Gardens of Heligan, Cornwall, England. This is reminiscent of Adrienne Lorkin's soul landscape, meandering through the foothills of the mountains, returning the traveller home.

How to dowse

Left Giulia Dence, a geopathic stress consultant, dowsing with metal rods.

Dowsing is an ancient method of detecting earth energies by using metal rods, a hazel fork or a pendulum. It is popularly known as a way of finding water, but in fact many different kinds of energy can be detected through dowsing.

These days dowsing is used by water boards, farmers, in mining explorations and more recently in office buildings, houses and gardens. Anyone can learn to do it, according to Christipher Bird in his book *The Divining Hand*, in which he cites the work of Dr. Zaboj V. Harvalik, a physicist and scientific advisor to the US Army's Advanced Materials Concepts Agency. Dr Harvalik concluded that dowsing works by transmitting energy through the adrenal glands to the pineal gland and it is then transmitted out through the muscles of the arms. The dowser is therefore the transmitter of the energy.

To dowse successfully it is a good idea to drink a glass of water beforehand, to prepare and clear yourself for some intuitive work. Stand holding the rods by your sides. Notice if you have too much tension in your shoulders and try to drop your energy into your lower body, so that your wrists and hands are loose enough to allow the rods to move freely.

Bend your arms at the elbows, making sure that the rods are parallel to the earth and not pointing downwards.

To ascertain whether if the rods cross they mean 'Yes' and when they are open they mean 'No' do a test dowse over a known site of the kind of energy you are looking for. For example, if you are dowsing for water, then test the rods over a pond, or even a bowl of water. If the rods work the other way round, that's ok, too. Just make sure that they are consistent.

Finally, be precise as to what you are looking for – a useful yardstick can be to consider whether the energy you are seeking is beneficial or detrimental, referring to the effects on our surroundings and ultimately our health.

So, Happy Dowsing, and one last thing – remember to 'switch off' from the dowsing frame of mind by sitting on the ground or having something to eat.

Resources

Garden design, consultation and training workshops

Pamela Woods BSc Hons, Dip. EGS at Sacred Gardens
Tel: 01453-885903
Web site:
www.sacredgardens.co.uk
Email: pamela@
sacredgardens.co.uk

Furniture and bespoke timberwork

Clever Decks and James Showers
Tel: 01453-885903

Garden Art
01453 756 361
Web site:
www.gardenart.co.uk

Arbor Vetum
Reclaimed teak furniture.
Tel: 01730-893000
Web site:
www.arborvetum.co.uk

Consultants

Giulia Dence BA KFRP
Health kinesiology and
Geopathic stress
consultancy and training.
Tel: 01453-889184
Email:
giuliadence@yahoo.co.uk

Helen Fletcher
Psychotherapy and healing.
Tel: 0113-278 0230
Email: HCFlet@CS.com

Artists

Tracy Whitbread
Painting – 'Power Flowers',
commissions undertaken.
Tel: 07748-132728
Email: www.tracy@
cloudcuckoo.freeserve.
co.uk

Janis Ridley
Sculpture – commissions
undertaken.
Tel: 01647-252099.

Alan Thornhill
Sculpture.
Tel: 01453-883673
Website:
www.alanthornhill.co.uk

John Glover
Garden photography.
Tel: 01428-751925
Email: john@glovphot.
demon.co.uk

Resources for green living

The Green Shop
Bisley, Gloucestershire.
Tel: 01452-770629

Gardens to visit in the UK

The Eden Project
St. Austell, Cornwall,
England.
Tel: 01726-811911

The Lost Gardens
of Heligan
St. Austell, Cornwall,
England.
Tel: 01726-845100

Tipton Lodge
Tipton St John,
East Devon, England.
By appointment and in
association with NCCPG.
Tel: Angie Avis on
01404-813371

The Chelsea Physic Garden
London, England.
Tel: 020-735 25646

The Garden History
Museum
London, England.
Tel: 020-7401 8865

Painshill Park
Surrey, England.
Tel: 01932-864674

Hadspen Garden
and Nursery
Castle Cary, Somerset,
England.
Tel: 01749-813707

The Chalice Well Gardens
Glastonbury, Somerset,
England.
Tel: 01458-831154

Gardens to visit in the USA

Esalen Gardens
The Esalen Institute,
Big Sur, California.

Cathedral of St. John
the Divine
New York, New York.

Green Gulch Farm
Zen Centre
Sausalito, California.

Hakone Japanese Garden
Saratoga, California.

Lilian Holt Center
for the Arts
Baltimore, Maryland.

Hume Japanese
Stroll Garden
Mill Neck, New York.

Mount Calvery Retreat
Santa Barbara, California.

Shyoan Teien
Middletown, Connecticut.

Zen Mountain House
Mt. Tremper, New York.

Further reading

Introduction
Topher Delany
Ten Landscapes
Rockport

Andy Goldsworthy
Time
Thames and Hudson

Derek Jarman's Garden
with photographs by
Howard Sooley
Thames and Hudson

Hamish Miller and
Paul Broadhirst
The Sun and the Serpent
Pendragon Press

Bruce Chatwin
The Songlines
Picador.

Robert Lawlor
Voices of the First Day
Inner Traditions

Paul Devereux and
Ian Thompson
*The Ley Hunters
Companion*
Thames and Hudson

Alfred Watkins
The Old Straight Track
Abacus

Garden energy
Jane Thurnell Read
*Geopathic Stress:
How earth energies
affect our lives*
Element

Gill Hale
The Feng Shui Garden
Aurum

Paul Devereux
The Sacred Place
Cassell and Co

Ancient Symbols
D. Lauren Artress
*Walking the Sacred Path –
Rediscovering the
Lanbyrinth as a Spiritual Tool*
NJ Putnam

Lucy R. Lippard
*Overlay – Contemporary Art
and the Art of Pre-history*
The New Press, New York

Marija Gimbutas
*The Language of
the Goddess*
Thames and Hudson

Aidan Meehan
Celtic Spirals
Thames and Hudson

Will Parfitt
The Living Qabala
Element

C.G. Jung
Man and His Symbols
Picador

Martin and Nigel Palmer
Sacred Britain
Piatkus

Adrian Fisher and George
Gerster
The Art of the Maze
Seven Dials

Universal patterns
Charles Jenks
*The Architecture of the
Jumping Universe*
Academy Editions

Ernst Haeckel
Art forms in Nature
Dover Publications, Inc. –
New York

John Briggs
*Fractals – the patterns
of Chaos*
Thames and Hudson

Richard Temple and Keith
Critchlow
The Golden Proportion
Parabola Winter Volume

A.T. Mann
Sacred Architecture
Element

Gary Zukav
The Dancing Wu Li Masters
Rider

Plant Spirit
Martín Prechtel
*Secrets of the
Talking Jaguar*
Tarcher/Putnam

Rupert Sheldrake
The Presence of the Past
Inner Traditions International

Valerie Anne Worwood
The Fragrant Pharmacy
Bantam Books

Patricia Davis
Subtle Aromatherapy
Daniel

Julian and Martine Barnard
*The Healing Herbs of
Edward Bach*
Bach Educational
Programme

The Findhorn Community
The Findhorn Garden
Findhorn Press

Nori and Sandra Pope
Colour by Design
Conran Octopus

Penelope Hobhouse
Colour in your Garden
Collins

Piet Oudolf
Designing with Plants
Conran Octopus

Jacqueline Memory
Patterson
Tree Wisdom
Thorsons

Going Deeper
Rae Beth
Hedgewitch
Robert Hale

Zsuzsanna E. Budapest
The Grandmother of Time
Harper Collins

Clarrisa Pinkola Estes
*Women Who Run With
the Wolves*
Rider

John Roulac
Backyard Composting
Green Earth Books

Derek Jarman
Modern Nature
Vintage

*The HDRA Encyclopaedia
of Organic Gardening*
The Henry DoubleDay
Research Association
Dorling Kindersley

Geoff Hamilton
The Organic Garden Book
Dorling Kindersley

David Pearson
Earth to Spirit
Gaia Books

Caroline Constant
The Woodland Cemetery
Byggforlaget, Syockholm.

Elizabeth Murray
Cultivating Sacred Space
Pomegranate

Machaelle Small Wright
*Garden Workbook –
A Complete Guide to
Gardening with Nature
Intelligences*
Warrenton, Va Perelandra.

Robert Lawlor Sacrde
*Geometry, Philosophy
and Practice*
Thames and Hudson

Wassily Kandinsky
*Concerning the
Spiritual in Art*
Dover

Index

Acknowledgements

Many, many thanks to all those friends who have seen me through this long process of writing my soul journey of creating gardens for the spirit. To John Glover, who pushed me to get started, and to Jan Winters, who lifted me up when the journey seemed to stop.

To all my clients who have happily allowed me to write about their own adventures in the making of their gardens.

To my wonderful, beautiful daughter who has always insisted that I put this work first and has given me plenty of loving and practical support. To my son who tracked down the best laptop for the job.

To all my teachers along the way who have inspired in me the mysteries of the worlds of spirit and indeed, to the plants themselves who have generously brought to me their wisdom and beauty, and to my Dad for his love of roses, the beginning of this journey for me.

To the fantastic team at Conran Octopus who have loved this book from start to finish. But most of all I want to thank my love James, who has always supported me with hundreds of cups of tea, many wonderful hot meals, but most of all with his infinite encouragement and belief in my work.
PAMELA WOODS

The publisher would like to thank the following photographers and agencies for their kind permission to reproduce the photographs in this book.
2-9 John Glover; 10 above Pamela Wood; 10 below John Glover; 11 Jerry Harpur (Design: Terry Welch, Seattle); 13–15 John Glover; 16 John Glover (Design: Landart); 17–21 John Glover; 22 John Glover (Design: Oudolf/Maynard); 23 John Glover; 24–25 John Glover (Design: Pamela Woods); 26–27 John Glover; 28–29 John Glover (Design: Pamela Woods); 30–31 John Glover; 32–33 John Glover (Design: Pamela Woods); 34–35 John Glover; 37 John Glover (Design: Pamela Woods); 38–40 John Glover; 41–42 John Glover (Design: Hamish Horsley); 43 John Glover (Design: Tom Stuart-Smith); 44 John Glover; 45 John Glover (Design: Ann Frith); 46 John Glover; 48–49 Land Artist and Photographer: Jim Buchanan; 50 John Glover (Design: Hamish Horsley); 51–52 John Glover; 53 right John Glover (Design: Pamela Woods); 55 John Glover; 56–56 John Glover (Design: Pamela Woods); 57 John Glover; 59–61 John Glover (Design: Pamela Woods); 62–67 John Glover; 68–69 John Glover (Maze: Adrian Fisher); 70 John Glover; 71 Jim Ballard/Getty Images; 72 John Glover (Design: Tim Brown); 73–75 John Glover; 77–79 John Glover (Design: Pamela Woods); 81 John Glover (Design: John Glover); 82–83 John Glover; 84 John Glover (Design: Pamela Woods); 85 John Glover; 86 Bill Ross/Corbis; 87 Ecoscene/Corbis; 88–89 John Glover; 90 John Blake/National Trust Photo Library; 91 Derek Croucher/National Trust Photo Library; 92–93 Jerry Harpur (Design: Terry Welch, Seattle); 94–106 John Glover; 107 Arnaud Descat/Mise au Point; 108–125 John Glover; 126–127 Ian Reeves/T. Delaney, Inc; 129–131 John Glover; 132 John Glover (Sculptor: Sharon Osmund); 133–145 John Glover; 146 John Glover (Design: Kristina Fitzsimmons); 147 John Glover (Design: Paul Riley); 148–161 John Glover
Every effort has been made to trace the copyright holders and we apologize in advance for any unintentional omission and would be pleased to insert the appropriate acknowledgement in any subsequent edition.